The
Best Ski Resorts in America

The
Best Ski Resorts in America

Claire Walter

Randt & Company, Inc.

First Edition

Library of Congress Cataloging-in-Publication Data

Walter, Claire.

    The best ski resorts in America.

    1. Ski resorts—United States.   2. Ski resorts—Canada. I. Title.
GV854.4.W33 1988   796.93'025'73   88-61159
ISBN 0-942101-03-0

Design and typesetting by Typographics, Ketchum, Idaho

Distributed to the trade by:
Kampmann & Company
New York, NY

Printed in the United States of America

10 9 8 7 6 5 4 3 2 1

To Abby Rand

The role model for all of us who love to ski
and write about it, and a good friend.

CONTENTS

The
Best Ski Resorts in America

Preface

For two decades, skiing has been my vocation and my pleasure, an enviable combination I share with just a few other journalists, feature writers, film makers, and editors. Skiing has taken me to places as different in style as New England and New Mexico, as different in climate as Canada and North Carolina, as different in scale as Connecticut, where the hills are gentle and rolling, and California, where mountains soar, as different in culture as Las Leñas, Argentina, and Les Diablerets, Switzerland.

I've crawled out of helicopters and climbed out of snowcats to ski mountains without a track on them. I've found ancient T-bars, which no one else wished to ride, to trails that were mine alone, and I've hustled onto hyper-modern high-speed quad chairlifts which fired skiers onto crowded slopes with BB-gun rapidity. I've skied bowls and bumps at huge destination resorts which attract fussy experts from all over the world, and I've skied humble hills around the corner where the joy of skiing is strictly low key and local. I've lost my mind under the awesome spell of panoramic mountains etched in high relief against a pure-blue sky, and I've lost my heart before a crackling fire in an old New England inn with snowflakes swirling outside small-paned windows.

Skiing friends, acquaintances, and even near-strangers who learn what I do for a living frequently ask me which is my favorite ski resort. And I always reply, truthfully, that I have no single favorite. Neither cruise ships nor tropical islands nor any other recreational destinations present themselves in the splendid variety offered by great ski resorts. There are intimate villages set against rugged mountains for purists whose only purpose is to get in the maximum number of runs per day—the steeper the terrain and deeper the powder, the better. There are gentle mountains groomed to make novices feel like intermediates, and intermediates feel like experts. And, of course, there are resorts where skiing for all ability levels is but one of the myriad pleasures. There are modern developments whose carefully planned buildings blend seamlessly with each other and with the surrounding woods, and there are patched-together towns that grew in a boom-or-bust fashion into places with quirky charm. There are resorts for questing swingles and others for staid families. And most remarkably, there are mega-resorts that have the magical quality of truly offering something for everyone.

In this book, I've tried to convey my understanding of the best mountains and best ski towns of North America, giving information and opinions about runs, lifts, lodgings, restaurants, and nightspots, while also providing an insight into the history and people that have made—and make—these resorts what they are. The goal of this book is to be a skiing experience in words and pictures that also affords a perspective on the best ski resorts in America—a perspective that is not only useful in choosing among the resorts but in enjoying the resorts that are chosen.

The information should be helpful whether you are a new skier or a veteran; whether you ski the machine-made snow of November or the loose corn of late spring; whether you go by yourself, as half of a couple, in a family, or with a group; or whether you are on a budget or not.

I am confident about what I describe because I've done all of the above and write about what I have experienced directly. I have chosen what I believe are the best ski resorts in America. They are areas with the best mountains and runs, and with the best facilities and services. As described in the following, everything in each resort may not be "the best," but each of the resorts has something of "the best" to offer.

Where skiers move around among ski areas that are in close proximity, I've grouped them into a single chapter. Therefore, while Colorado's Breckenridge, Copper Mountain, and Keystone each could merit an individual chapter, vacationers bounce among them on a "Ski the Summit" lift ticket—and therefore, they appear together in this book. The same goes for the Tahoe resorts of California, the "Ski 93" group in New Hampshire, Utah's Park City areas, and the four ski mountains of Aspen, Colorado.

Any mention of people who made this book possible must begin with Dana and Gina Randt, who gave me the highest compliment by asking me to write my dream book for their new publishing company and who have supported it with the enthusiasm that could come only from fellow skiers. To those in the ski industry whose tracks I've crossed over the years, I owe the greatest appreciation. My gratitude especially goes to the public relations and marketing executives at ski areas and resort associations across the continent who have been so helpful for so many years, along with the legions of ski school directors, ski instructors, operations managers, nursery supervisors, and innkeepers who have given so generously of their time and insights. A list would comprise another chapter, so thanks, gang. You know who you are.

Claire Walter

Early Years

The roots of American skiing are in European soil: in Scandinavia, where people have used cross-country skis for winter transportation for a thousand years, and in the Alps, where mountain men began turning skiing into a downhill sport a century ago. Scandinavian immigrants brought skiing to the Midwest, the California goldfields, and the Rockies.

The first documented use of skis in the United States was in 1841 in Wisconsin, an area heavily populated by Norwegians. In the 1850s and sixties in California, the legendary John A. "Snowshoe" Thompson was skiing the mail over the mountains to isolated mining camps, where skiing had become one of the few winter diversions. Ski competitions became common, featuring wild downhill races on devilish twelve-foot skis with a single long pole for steering and braking.

While western skiing was a working man's sport practiced by miners and farmers, eastern skiing was an activity of the elite. In New York's Adirondack Mountains, where bluebloods were used to spending their summers, the baronial Lake Placid Club stayed open during the winter of 1904-5 for ice skating and skiing. Five years later, to promote ski competition among well-connected collegians, the Dartmouth Outing Club was created in Hanover, New Hampshire. The first inter-

*Early skiing in
the northern Rockies*

collegiate meet took place in 1913 between Dartmouth and Montreal's McGill University. In 1927, Dartmouth's Winter Meet, a forerunner of the present Dartmouth Winter Carnival, included its first downhill race, along the old Mount Moosilauke Carriage Road.

While Scandinavian-Americans were sliding around in the high Sierra and elsewhere in America, an eccentric Austrian genius named Mathias Zdarsky was so inspired by stories of a man who had travelled across Greenland on skis that he ordered a pair for himself. Because the skis arrived with no directions, Zdarsky had to invent his own technique. Skiing down the sloping pastureland surrounding Lilienfeld, his town in the Alps' eastern foothills, not far from Vienna, Zdarsky not only developed the technique of using two poles instead of one, but also created the snowplow and stem turns which are now the rudiments of modern Alpine technique. Finally Zdarsky began to teach skiing.

To the west in 1907, Viktor Sohm started the first organized ski school in Zürs, a small hamlet in Austria's Arlberg, an isolated region of high Alps and small farming villages closer to Switzerland than to Vienna and Lilienfeld. Hannes Schneider, however, would become the most enduringly famous Arlberg ski instructor. When he was young, his father wanted him to become a cheesemaker, but instead, he chose to work for Viktor Sohm. After World War I, Schneider developed a ski-teaching progression that revolutionized ski instruction. Schneider took Zdarsky's technique, refined it, and codified it into a systematic method that came to be known as the Arlberg Technique. One of Schneider's many successful and enthusiastic students was Katherine Peckett, the daughter of a prominent New Hampshire hotel owner. She was so taken with the potential of skiing as a winter sport that she recruited Austrian instructors to teach skiing in the White Mountains in the United States.

Sig Buchmayer began as an instructor at Peckett's in 1929, the first of the influential Austrians who brought the Arlberg Technique and modern skiing to America in the thirties. Others included Otto Schniebs at Dartmouth; Hans Thorner, first at Lake Placid and later at Cannon Mountain, New Hampshire; Otto Lang at Mount Ranier, Washington; Sepp Ruschp at Stowe, Vermont; Hans Hauser at Sun Valley, Idaho; Friedl Pfeifer, first at Sun Valley and later at Aspen, Colorado; Hannes Schroll and Luggi Foeger at Sugar Bowl, California; and Benno Rybizka at North Conway, New Hampshire. In 1939, Hannes Schneider himself came to the United States. Imprisoned by the Nazis for protesting the German annexation of Austria, Schneider was released upon the personal intercession of Harvey Gibson, a ski enthusiast, president of Manufacturers Trust Company, and founder of Mount Cranmore at North Conway, New Hampshire.

Concurrent with the Austrian skiing invasion was the development of ski lifts of all kinds. Whether skiers were beginners learning the sport on a gentle meadow beside Peckett's or experts skiing in early downhill races, the one thing they almost all had in common was that they walked up every vertical foot that they ultimately skied down. A few primitive lifts, rigged by imaginative mining engineers, had appeared in the early years of the century. Sierra skiers were known to have ridden in ore buckets in the 1800s, and a lift consisting of two toboggans attached to a rope loop and powered by a steam engine was in operation near Truckee on the North Shore of Lake Tahoe in 1913. But these were the rare exceptions.

Twenty years and a lot of climbing later, the first rope tow in North America began operating at Shawbridge, Quebec. While it now may seem as if a rope tow was a step backward, in reality it represented progress. The rope tow was quicker, more efficient, and less expensive than anything

The first chairlift in the world was built in Sun Valley, Idaho.

else that had been used before.

In the thirties lift technology underwent rapid advancement. The first rope tow in the United States began operating on Gilbert's Hill near Woodstock, Vermont, in 1934. So popular was this tow that several more were soon installed at nearby Suicide Six, a steep little hill with a mean pitch. One Harold Codding set a record of thirty round trips in an hour on the 650 vertical feet of Suicide Six. While the development and use of the rope tow set off the first American ski boom, skiers and inventors continued to experiment with other kinds of tows. A more sophisticated toboggan-type was built at Sugar Bowl in 1934; the Dartmouth Outing Club installed a J-bar on Oak Hill the following year; and in 1941, the world's first T-bar went in at Pico Peak, near Rutland, Vermont.

But the most significant single development of this period was the invention of the chairlift and its installation at Sun Valley. James Curran, a non-skiing but visionary engineer, saw the future of uphill transport in a derivation of the cable hoists which were used to load bunches of bananas into the cargo holds of fruit boats. Charlie Proctor, a former Dartmouth racer who was employed to lay out Sun

The Tenth Mountain Division,
Camp Hale, Colorado.

Valley's ski terrain, was intrigued by Curran's idea of hanging chairs from a continuously moving cable—and so was Averell Harriman, the Union Pacific Railroad chairman who caused Sun Valley to be built.

Harriman finally approved the plans for the first chairlift, which was built in 1936 with the awesome uphill capacity of 450 skiers an hour. Subsequently, Gunstock, New Hampshire, and Stowe, Vermont, had the first chairlifts in the East, and Sugar Bowl the first in California. And soon after the end of World War II, the first double chairlift was erected at Mount Spokane, Washington.

The postwar years were boom times. The Army's Tenth Mountain Division, located at Camp Hale, Colorado, had trained 10,000 ski troops, using as instructors an assortment of former college ski racers, expatriate Europeans, and members of the then young National Ski Patrol System. When these soldiers, who had a love of the mountains and a knowledge of skiing, were released into civilian life, the ski industry began in earnest.

Technology also helped to make skiing easier and more accessible, with aircraft engineers responsible for some of skiing's most far-reaching advances. Art Hunt, Wayne Pierce, and James Richey of the Chance Vought Aircraft Company came up not only with the first functioning gun for snow-making but also with the Alu 60, one of the first all-metal skis in the world. The Alu was heavy and impractical because its metal base tended to stick in wet snow, but it set another aircraft engineer to thinking and tinkering. Howard Head made a remarkable ski of aluminum sandwiching a wood core. He added a plastic running surface and steel edges—and revolutionized skiing. Head's lightweight, maneuverable ski made skiing easier and more fun. Equipment developments followed with breathtaking speed in the fifties and sixties. Wood skis gave way to metal, and metal soon gave way to fiberglass. Leather boots were replaced by leather buckle boots, which soon were glazed with plastic to make them waterproof. Before long, boots were composed of plastic shells lined with an array of materials designed to mold to the wearer's feet. Rear-entry boots, high-back racing boots, and even heated boots followed.

Binding technology also became highly sophisticated. Pre-war contraptions of leather and metal were replaced by cable bindings, consisting of a pivoting toepiece and a cable to hold down the heel. Then a variety of releasable bindings appeared, including plate bindings and even toeless models. Poles became lighter and stronger. And space-age synthetics made skiwear warmer, dryer, and more fashionable.

On the mountains, chairlifts of all sorts became the norm. Where a single chair had once been cause for wonder, there are now doubles, triples, quads, high-speed detachable quads, and state-of-the-art gondolas and trams. And no major eastern or midwestern ski area exists without snowmaking, a magical combination of art, science, and witchcraft that creates dense, packable, groomable snow from a mixture of compressed air and water, and makes skiers less dependent on the weather. Slope grooming likewise has become a high art, with fleets of $100,000-plus snowcats working through the night, preparing the mountain for the following day.

Nowadays, the best ski resorts in America present a broad spectrum of skiing and vacation experience. Terrain ranges from tough and demanding to gentle and forgiving; accommodations, from spartan and efficient—as they are in the heli-ski resorts of Canada—to fantastic and nearly excessive, as they are in some of the resorts in the Rockies. And the types of people who go to these resorts are also different.

With jet planes and interstate highways, most of these areas are no more than a day's trip away, no matter where one is in North America. But before you book your next flight, look at some photographs and let me tell you about these resorts.

Aspen, Colorado

ASPEN IS ON THE SAME
JET-SET WAVELENGTH AS
BEVERLY HILLS OR ST TROPEZ

Aspen is a town, a mountain, and a state of mind. It is to skiers what Mecca is to Moslems. It is also the standard by which all other ski resorts are judged. Aspen has it all. It is a gorgeous town with great skiing, fabulous dining, inspiring cultural activities, splendid shopping, and rollicking nightlife.

Aspen attracts the ultra-establishment (former Secretary of Defense and World Bank President Robert McNamara) and the anti-establishment (gonzo journalist Hunter Thompson). It boasts jocks (former downhill racer Andy Mill, who married Chris Evert) and thinkers (the intellectuals of the Aspen Institute for Humanistic Studies). It is a place where ski bums live like sardines in outlying trailer parks, while show-biz types (Jill St. John, Jack Nicholson, Barbara Mandrell, Buddy Hackett, and the like) roost in multi-million-dollar chalets on Red Mountain. Aspen is Learjets and pickup trucks, ankle-length mink coats and latter-day-hippie fringed leather vests, sushi with sake, and chili with Coors.

The town has grown around so chic, wealthy, and, yes, wild a core that it is on the same jet-set wavelength as Beverly Hills or St. Tropez. Despite the eclectic nature of the Aspen skier popula-

*Woodrun Place in Snowmass is
a convenient slopeside condo-hotel.*

tion, "rich" carries the dominant genes, and consumption is conspicuous. Aspen is hedonistic high living, but most of all, it is skiing on four mountains that rank with the best in the world.

SKIING

Mighty Aspen Mountain, which locals call Ajax after an old mining claim, stands like a wall of white, right next to town. The best known of the four mountains of Aspen, it is composed of three steep ridges and the gullies between them. Into this area seventy trails, totalling twenty-three miles in length, have been cut on a 3,267-foot vertical.

The beefiest of these ridges—the center one—is Bell Mountain. Powderhounds drop down the steep eastern flank and lose themselves in such tight, ungroomable glades as Face of Bell and Shoulder of Bell, Christmas Tree, and Keith Glen on the western side. Those whose technique in the bumps is worth watching may play on Ridge of Bell, a heart-stopping double-black-diamond run in full view of skiers both on the gondola and the old Bell Mountain double chair.

Snowmass offers excellent cruising on 1,560 skiable acres.

International and Ruthie's Run glaze the top of the easternmost ridge, but it is the half-dozen short, steep fall-aways—which have names like Bear Paw, Short Snort, and Zaugg, though they really are just the most-skied paths through the woods—that provide the real excitement. The most recently developed sector, Gentleman's Ridge, which is to the west, has a combination of long, sinuous trails and shorter bumped-up steeps. For powder getaways, there is also snowcat skiing in 1,400 acres of paradisiacal hidden bowls.

If the Buttermilk/Tiehack area were anyplace else in the country, it would be a worthy destination in its own right. Two connected peaks, with 2,030 feet of vertical, feature gentle meadows, long cruising trails, powder-holding glades and a mountaintop bowl of respectable proportions. But located two miles from Aspen, it is regarded as a bunny hill. And in fact it has been transformed into a learning center where Vic Braden, the irrepressible guru of tennis instruction, has founded America's first ski-learning research center. His goal, using willing Aspen skiers, is to create a new instructional method. Buttermilk also offers a Fit-For-Life program that combines ski instruction and change of habits for people over fifty who wish to continue an active lifestyle.

Next door is Aspen Highlands. At 3,800 vertical feet, it is the country's second-highest ski mountain. There are broad beginner slopes, wide blue-square smoothies, bumped-up fall-line runs, and a razor-back ridge. With awesome vistas that unfold layer upon layer as you ride up a series of lifts to the 11,800-foot summit, the Highlands bills itself as the best-kept secret in Aspen, which is an accurate, if somewhat unhappy, slogan. The mountain has logged fewer than 200,000 skier visits during its best ski season—far fewer than Vail handles during the Christmas holidays alone.

The Highlands experience is short on glamour and long on friendliness, with skiing on the old-fashioned side—old lifts provide a leisurely ride up a quirky mountain that never has been the subject of computerized trail planning. But slow lifts don't matter very much because the only lift lines you'll ever encounter are for the chairs accessing the more challenging upper mountain runs, but even then the lines are not very long. The Loges Peak chair is one of skiing's must-take lift rides. It skims the razorback, dips dazzlingly into a mid-ride hollow, and offers sensational views. And there is one relatively easy route down.

Twelve miles from town is Snowmass, a modern resort that combines convenient slopeside lodging with perhaps the best intermediate skiing in America. While the terrain of each of the two other big mountains, Ajax and Highlands, thrusts deeply back from a narrow base to a narrower peak, Snowmass sprawls horizontally as well as vertically (its base-to-summit vertical measures out to 3,615 feet). More than fifty-five miles of runs—1,582 eminently skiable acres—are spread over four humpy mountains.

While Snowmass has steeps (off the Campground chair and the mountaintop Hanging Valley Glades), it is particularly well suited for recreational skiers who want to cruise, cruise, and cruise some more. Long, wide, immaculately groomed runs without peer in quality and quantity predominate across this vast ski area. When Snowmass was created, its signature run was the Big Burn, a moderately pitched mega-slope. Now, the area has been around for a while and the saplings of the early years have grown, so the Burn has become more like an open glade with widely spaced trees, but it remains the most splendid ego skiing imaginable. And time has also brought lift development. Three detachable quad chairs, including one uncorking the base-area bottleneck on Fanny Hill and one on the Burn, have recently upped the Snowmass lift capacity to over 20,500 skiers an hour.

Three of these four ski areas are owned by the Aspen Skiing Company and can be skied with a fully interchangeable lift ticket. Aspen Highlands, which is not one of the three, sued the Aspen Skiing Company to mandate an all-Aspen pass. The case made it all the way to the Supreme Court, where Highlands won; an optional four-area coupon book is now available.

HISTORY

Aspen was almost a ghost town in the 1930s when a small group of enthusiastic skiers laid claim to the snow-covered, sun-kissed mountains from which some of the richest silver ore had once been mined. They formed a ski club and in 1936 imported André Roch from Switzerland to pick the most skiable mountain. After he selected Aspen Mountain, just north of town, club members cut a trail and named it Roch Run, which still exists today. An early lift, called a boat tow, consisting of two sleds on a cable powered by a truck engine, was constructed to carry skiers uphill.

Substantial development began after the war. In 1946, industrialist Walter Paepcke founded the Aspen Skiing Corporation, and within a few years he was able to transform the desolate mining town beside the Roaring Fork River into America's top place to ski, though during the next four decades, the resort has had its ups and downs.

In 1950, Aspen was put on the international map when it became the site of the World Alpine Championships, the first time this prestigious event was held in North America. After hearing about Aspen, people kept coming, first by train and later by bus, car, and plane. Aspen soon became known as *the* skiers' mountain. These were the glory years in the Roaring Fork Valley. Abandoned buildings were reclaimed and a slew of new lodges appeared at the base of the mountain. The seeds of Aspen's vibrant nightlife were sown early by guests and residents alike who seemed to have boundless energy.

In 1958, Friedl Pfeifer, who was Aspen Mountain's first ski school director, opened Buttermilk as a training ground for skiing Ajax's steeps. At about the same time, a Philadelphian named Whipple Van Ness Jones began to develop Aspen Highlands as an independent ski area. But even with these facilities, the crowds overflowed. As a result, the Aspen Skiing Corporation and the Janss

Corporation (of Sun Valley fame) embarked on a new venture that changed the face of skiing in America. Snowmass-at-Aspen opened in 1967, with the hope that some of Aspen's cachet would rub off on the new project. But once people started skiing Snowmass, it stood on its own. Nothing else in skidom had the long wide trails with which Snowmass debuted. The master stroke was the construction of a lift up the Big Burn, a half-mile-wide swath cleared by an ancient forest fire. The Burn has something for everyone. Novices traverse it safely. Intermediates savor the fabulous ego-skiing that encourages non-stop rhythmic turns. And even Aspen's fussiest experts head for the highly rated powder on the Burn after a snowfall.

But as Snowmass was expanding, with new terrain and new lodging every year, the first signs of trouble appeared in Aspen. In the late sixties the counterculture was in full bloom in Aspen, and just as many of the local drifters were turning on, many ski enthusiasts were turning off. Families, avoiding a growing downtown scene of scruff laced with drugs, found Snowmass more congenial. Although the America's Downhill became a regular World Cup stop on Aspen Mountain and the Winterskol festival generated business during the January doldrums, Aspen kept losing ground to upstart Snowmass. Many downtown lodges got shabby, and the resort's popularity eroded.

While newer resorts elsewhere in the Rockies were developing terrain in the Snowmass mode, installing modern lifts and creating communities that owed more to Disneyland than to resurrected mining towns, Aspen was left fallow. The Aspen Skiing Corporation changed hands a few times, eventually becoming the Aspen Skiing Company, but little was done to upgrade its mountains. As a result, Vail overtook Aspen as the number-one destination ski resort in America.

Recovering from that shock meant starting from square one. The town of Aspen cleaned up its act, and so did the mountain company. The first two quad chairs were installed on Ajax in 1985-86, but the next season was the turn-around year. During the venerable mountain's glowing fortieth-anniversary season, the year-old Buckhorn fixed-grip quad was converted to a detachable, and a four-seater was installed on Little Nell.

In addition, the Silver Queen made its debut: A six-passenger gondola, it reduces the time from the bottom of Little Nell to Ajax's apex from thirty-two to thirteen minutes. Skiers who had forsaken Aspen Mountain for Snowmass began to return. Locals have come back for the demanding skiing, and visitors have started taking early lunches on the Sundeck or in the elegant sitdown dining room at the renovated Ruthie's Restaurant. Aspen Mountain has regained its edge.

LODGING

Along with mountain improvements, a frenzied spring cleaning has taken place all over town, with a third of the lodgings upgraded. Joining the growing list of upscale accommodations were the Hotel Lenado, a luxury lodge in a rustic contemporary style; the Independence Square Hotel, with bright rustic furniture and an eye-popping rooftop Jacuzzi; the Sardy House, a gracious Victorian boutique hotel; and the Inn at Aspen, which has a swim-up Jacuzzi bar. The Wheeler Opera House was totally restored and now adds a festive note to downtown Aspen. And one of the most dramatic comeback stories has been the Hotel Jerome, a landmark that embodies Aspen's checkered past. The hotel went into a slow decline that reached its nadir in the sixties, when Aspen was a hippie haven and the Jerome was painted purple. Only the Jerome Bar remained a popular hangout. In 1986, however, $4.5 million was spent to refurbish the hotel, which had been built for $125,000 a century earlier. The Jerome now sparkles with etched-glass light fixtures, polished marble, shining woodwork, and precious furnishings. Accommodations have been changed from sixty spartan cubbyholes to twenty-eight spacious rooms. Today, the Jerome is a contemporary triumph as well as a historic landmark.

RESTAURANTS AND APRÈS-SKI

Aspen must be considered America's après-ski capital, for it attracts party people of so many different stripes. Pretty girls and pretty boys with Pepsodent smiles gleaming from tanned faces can be found almost everywhere, along with men escaping mid-life crises and well-off women who are bored with shopping. Some vacationers just watch; some accelerate and move into the scene briefly during their stay, while still others are so enraptured that they shift into overdrive and stay forever.

Après-ski is a moveable feast, and it almost doesn't matter where the "in" crowd is during any given season, though après-ski traditionally has started on the terrace of Little Nell's, and continued through the night at the Jerome Bar, O'Leary's, The Tippler, and dozens of other watering holes.

Snowmass has its own much milder après-ski scene. The Timber Mill, its deck now moved to slopeside, is the first stop, while the Tower is popular with families who dominate the resort, for the bartenders are as adept at magic tricks as in mixing a margarita—or a Shirley Temple.

Aspen has more than a hundred places to eat, from fast-food outlets to serious gourmet restaurants. Long-established spots include André's, The Golden Horn, and Guido's, all known for excellent continental cuisine; La Cocina and Toro's for affordable Mexican; or the Aspen Mine Company, Cooper Street Downstairs, and the Skier's Chalet for steaks and other grilled specialties. The Crystal Palace does funny, irreverent satirical dinner theater, while the Grand Finale serves dinner followed by a Broadway show. And there's dancing at Little Annie's and The Tippler. But for good food, super après-ski, and a trendy crowd, Abetone is the current in-spot with a busy bar and a lovely restaurant serving first-rate northern Italian cuisine.

OTHER ACTIVITIES

While Aspen's mountains offer world-class skiing, it is astonishing that a third of the winter visitors never ride a lift or cruise downhill. They may ski cross-country at Ashcroft, take a dogsled ride at Krabloonik, glide over the Roaring Fork Valley in a hot-air balloon, rent a snowmobile at the T-Lazy-7 Ranch, play tennis or do aerobics at the classy Snowmass Club or classier Aspen Club, gallery-hop, shop, or study Oriental martial arts.

It is doubtful that Aspen can ever again overtake Vail in sheer numbers; it is too far from Denver to get much weekend business. But Aspen, having completed what it calls its "second renaissance," is looking better than ever. Still, or again, Aspen is the place to be.

Jackson Hole, Wyoming

JACKSON HOLE IS THE
QUINTESSENTIAL WILD WEST
SKI RESORT

Among the trappers and fur traders who used to work the Tetons in the early 1800s was a mountain man named Davey Jackson. He inhabited a high valley, or "hole," that came to be known as Jackson Hole.

Jackson Hole is now the quintessential Wild West ski resort, both in terms of ultra-expert skiing and of the Stetson-and-stirrups ambiance of the nearby town of Jackson. Located in the remote Teton range of the Rocky Mountains, which looms like a craggy wall above a broad, flat valley, Jackson Hole is unique. This mega-ski area measures nearly 3,000 skiable acres, with a 4,139-foot vertical, and an incredible three-mile stretch across the top, which made it the country's biggest ski area until Vail's expansion in 1988-89. It is also unquestionably one of the best.

While most other ski areas make do with three trail signs (the familiar green circle, blue square, and black diamond) to indicate levels of difficulty, Jackson Hole from the outset has seen a need for five: the usual three, plus a red square which designates an upper-advanced run, and a bright red exclamation point within a red triangle against a yellow background, which means *ultra*-expert—unless you can handle maximum steepness under any snow conditions, keep off.

Figure 8s in Cody Bowl.

The usual non-ski opportunities in this corner of northwestern Wyoming are also peerless, with sleighrides to the National Elk Refuge, where there are 7,500 head of elk, and snowmobiling through Yellowstone Park to Old Faithful. And the rowdy, irreverent atmosphere of the town of Jackson at night is a contrast to quiet Teton Village, the huddle of lodges at the base of the ski area.

Today, Jackson Hole's skiing stretches across two adjacent mountains: mighty Rendezvous for maximum challenge; and Après Vous, the 2,140-vertical-foot bunny hill. Crystal Springs is the mostly intermediate valley between them. If it stood alone rather than in the long shadow cast by Rendezvous, Après Vous would be considered an enchanting playground of well-groomed novice and intermediate runs. But, because Jackson Hole is so difficult to reach, expert skiers come for Rendevous' heart-stopping steeps and almost limitless bowls. Après Vous is used by spouses, children, and friends.

When Jackson Hole was developed for skiing in 1965, a tramway was constructed to the summit. Every twelve minutes, sixty-three skiers would disembark and have America's then biggest ski mountain to themselves. It was like heli-skiing without the helicopter—endless stretches of untracked snowfields, radical chutes, pristine bowls, and near-solitude—and the tram rarely got grounded by inclement weather. Lifts have since been added to access the upper mountain. First

The National Elk Refuge is bordered by the Grand Tetons.

the Thunder Chair was strung up on Rendezvous' northern edge, accessing even the most demanding chutes. In 1987-88, a quad chair was put in to serve the bowls on the southern part of the *massif*, and a high-speed Poma was installed to the very top. Even with these additions, however, Rendezvous remains relatively uncrowded.

SKIING

A skier's first experience at Jackson Hole should be from the tram on a clear day. It takes just seven minutes to go 2.4 miles from Teton Village to the top of the world. The vista from the summit is awe-inspiring. The jagged high peaks of the majestic Grand Tetons stretch off in both directions, and beyond the flat ranchland that flanks the Snake River more than 4,000 feet below is the splendor of the Gros Ventre Range. The white splendor of Rendezvous Peak and the ski terrain stretch temptingly below.

There are two options from the top of the tram. One is to slide off the cornice into Rendezvous Bowl, a black-diamond cirque that is manageable even by strong intermediates because it is wide enough to traverse. The second option—not recommended—is to attempt Corbet's Couloir. Super experts, imbued with commando courage and exceptional skill, leap over an awesome precipice between walls of rock to ski a slope that exceeds 45 degrees. It's a bit like jumping into an elevator shaft. Skiers with the merest shred of common sense can use a rope to lower themselves off the ledge and into the chute, but they still have to be terribly good to take it from there.

Below the top section, the mountain unfolds layer by layer. The Rendezvous Trail cutoff leads southward from the top of Rendezvous Bowl, toward the new quad and beyond to Cheyenne and Laramie Bowls. Cheyenne is Jackson's widest bowl—and one of its gentlest. Laramie is a somewhat elongated version, wide at the top and then funneling into a steeper gully below. Anyone who's sorry to have missed the thrills and chills of Corbet's can also enter Laramie via the perilous Alta Chutes. Another option is the short, near vertical run nicknamed Toilet Bowl. It's not on the map, and its access, near Tram Tower Three, is easy to miss. With it's 33 percent average pitch and monster moguls, it's never forgotten by those who find it.

With the Thunder Chair, upgraded for higher capacity, and the new quad, it is now possible to ski nothing but these high bowls all day. Skiers who prefer summit-to-base skiing proceed down to one of five long ridges and deep gullies that lead to the base; these are black-diamond runs with steady pitches and wide glades. From there, one can either head over to Après Vous via the gentle Union Pass Traverse or go back up the tram for another round with the big mountain.

Still another route from the summit is to cross over to the Hobacks. This is a mile-long steadily pitched slope, rippled with two ridges and two long gullies. This is Jackson's best powder preserve, dotted sparsely with trees and altogether sensational.

Intermediate skiers doing the big mountain once just for the experience can take their time on Rendezvous Bowl and then follow the South Pass Traverse to the blue squares in Casper Bowl and Après Vous. It is now also possible to ski all runs on Rendezvous Mountain without riding the tram—or enduring the tram waits. Skiers may take the Crystal Springs, Cascade, and Thunder chairs and then the new high-speed Poma lift all the way to the top.

Jackson Hole visitors tick off vertical feet on Rendezvous just as heli-skiers do. The ski area contributes to their boasting rights by distributing a logbook and awarding certificates for 100,000 or 150,000 vertical feet skied in a week. Bronze, silver, and gold Western-style belt buckles are given for respective *lifetime* totals of 300,000, 500,000 and 1,500,000 vertical feet.

Despite its reputation for extreme skiing, Jackson Hole is, in reality, a good place to learn to ski. After all, with most of the gung-ho skiers up on Rendezvous, low-level classes aren't mobbed. The ski school, run by the Austrian-born former Olympic gold medalist Pepi Stiegler, is excellent. Jackson Hole was one of the eight ski areas that were used as a testing ground for NASTAR racing in the late sixties, and for years Stiegler was the country's zero-handicap pacesetter, besting men half his age. He can still beat the down car of the tram to the bottom.

As one of the country's toughest ski mountains, Jackson Hole gets the best skiers. The top powder technicians annually compete in the Figure 8 contest, testing which team of two can lay down the most perfectly synchronized tracks on an out-of-bounds bowl. The Iron Skier Triathlon is a relatively new ultrasport played out at Jackson Hole. This grueling competition starts with a harrowing three-mile schuss across challenging out-of-bounds terrain (which includes the rubble of an avalanche path) followed by a one-mile uphill run at 10,000 feet above sea level and finishes with a leap into Corbet's for the seven-mile downhill to the valley.

The typical Jackson Hole experience, however, can certainly be shared by casual recreational skiers. Many like to mix playing on the plenitude of easier terrain with swimming in outdoor pools, with cross-country skiing, or with excursions through the magnificent high-mountain country.

APRÈS-SKI

Everybody but everybody staying at the ski area goes to Jackson for at least one night on the town, most for several nights. At the Million Dollar Cowboy Bar, patrons divide their time between the dance floor and bar stools shaped like saddles. At the Silver Dollar Bar in the Wort Hotel, more than two thousand real silver dollars are embedded in the forty-six-foot-long bar top. Visitors never tire of the rollicking, stomping, high-energy atmosphere of these big, busy nightspots. More melodious music is found at the Rancher Bar, where forties' tunes are played. To mingle with the locals, savvy après-skiers head for the Shady Lady, where the reggae is hot and the company is cool.

LODGING AND RESTAURANTS

The most convenient accommodations are at Teton Village at the base of the ski area. Nestling up to the clock tower are just five lodges. On either end are the Alpenhof and the Hostel. The former is the most luxurious, a Bavarian-style inn with considerable charm and the best restaurant in the village, the elegant Garden Room, serving continental and upscale-American cuisine. The most economical is the Hostel, the choice of thrifty families and bunk-room dwellers. Its restaurant, the Buffalo Pit, encourages guests to grill their own steaks, and its large lounge is a popular, casual gathering place. Between these hotels, are Teton Village's moderately priced lodges: the Inn at Jackson Hole, Sojourner Inn, and the tiny Crystal Springs Inn. Completing the village are the Village Center Inn, a condo-hotel next to the tram terminal, and seven condo complexes nestled in the trees. Some are within walking distance of the lifts; others require shuttle-bus use.

Some of the best-appointed properties are off-campus. The Jackson Hole Racquet Club just a few miles down the road is a complete resort with plenty of activities even for non-skiers. Amenities include a health club with Nautilus, free weights, saunas, whirlpool, steamroom, and tanning beds; three indoor tennis courts; racquetball; a gym for pickup basketball and volleyball; indoor running track; and outdoor ice skating. Stiegler's, a fine Austrian restaurant, is also on site. A newer, no less luxurious complex is the Spring Creek Ranch with cross-country skiing, skating, and outdoor hot tub. The Granary, one of the best restaurants in the area, offers a rotating selection of four-course *prix fixe* dinners.

In Jackson, the Snow King Resort is the biggest hotel, with heated outdoor swimming pool, hot tub, sauna, cross-country skiing, and its own 1,571-vertical-foot ski mountain with two chairlifts and night skiing Wednesdays through Saturdays. The best-known of the downtown properties is the old Wort Hotel. Its rooms are now contemporary, but its traditional status as the hub of Jackson remains, and its Goldpiece Room serves trendy American fare. Even trendier is the nearby Cadillac Grille, a retro-look watering hole with a sparkling ambiance and excellent food.

The mental picture of Jackson that visitors take home is of a massive mountain, its spectacular steeps buried in white powder. But there is much more to Jackson, which is a memory well worth having.

Killington, Vermont

KILLINGTON RANKS WITH VAIL
AND MAMMOTH MOUNTAIN
IN ANNUAL SKIER VISITS

Killington, a mega-mountain in central Vermont, is all the superlatives of eastern skiing wrapped up in one package. Its vertical (3,060 feet) is the greatest in New England and, after Whiteface Mountain, New York, the second highest in the East. It has more skiable mountains (6 interconnected peaks), more trails (107), more acreage (721), more base lodges (6, plus one summit lodge), more lifts (18), and more uphill capacity (over 30,000 skiers an hour) than any other ski area east of the Rockies. Its gondola (3.5 miles) is the longest ski lift in North America, and its Juggernaut trail (10 miles) is the continent's longest. Killington also has more snowmaking (on 66 trails, over 40 miles) and one of the longest ski seasons in the East. The earliest opening was October 12, 1987, and the latest closing was June 21, 1984. Spread across a *massif* in the heart of the Green Mountains, it is big, sometimes intimidating, but never boring.

Located within weekend driving distance of much of the northeastern megalopolis (three-and-a-half hours from Boston, five-and-a-half from New York, and seven from Philadelphia), Killington's priority has been to offer skiing for everyone. Killington was never known for friendliness and service, for lovely ambiance, or even for a New England image. It *has* been known for efficiency,

At 3.5 miles the gondola at Killington is the longest lift in North America.

innovative multi-day package pricing, and most important, reliable skiing. While other ski areas were putting the proverbial cart before the horse—building condos, pedestrian malls, and pretty clock towers—Killington was putting its money into more lifts, more snow-making, and more trail-maintenance equipment. The company knows it is in the ski business, not the real estate, the hotel, the health-spa, the fitness-center, or the indoor-tennis business. At Killington skiing came first, and the rest of the niceties followed. New slope-side building complexes have been undertaken by top developers, despite opposition from the State of Vermont, which seems bent on curtailing ski-resort growth, particularly at Killington.

But the area, less than thirty years old, has the momentum of steady growth behind it. In 1959, an energetic young entrepreneur named Preston Leete Smith, a descendent of a pre-Revolutionary governor of Connecticut, launched his ski empire with just three Pomalifts, a tarpaper-roofed base lodge, an eight-hole outhouse as the sole amenity, and traditional New England trails: rock-ribbed runs that combined narrowness and pitch. The area's earliest seasons preceded the great ski boom of the sixties, and, in fact, Killington deserves credit as one of the fuses that detonated the boom. At that time when most classic New England areas were still a web of steep, rocky trails snaking off wind-blown mountaintops, Killington's first major expansion was to a 530-vertical-foot knoblet dubbed Snowshed. It was, and remains, a wide gentle slope ideal for learning to ski. Who knows how many thousands of skiers have taken their first lessons on this unprepossessing bump?

With dreams of building a mountain of unprecedented size, Smith directed Killington to the leading edge of ski instruction. In the late sixties, in the trial-and-error evolution of ski instruction techniques, Killington's Snowshed was the testing ground for the Graduated Length Method, where adult beginners started on three-footers and graduated incrementally to normal-length skis. When this approach fell out of favor because it gave skiers a false sense of skill without the underpinnings of basic technique, Killington replaced it with the Accelerated Ski Method. ASM modified the best of classic ski progression with some of the shortcuts and ego-pleasing techniques of GLM. Snowshed is now served by one high-speed quad, two double chairlifts, and a Pomalift, and Killington's 150-instructor ski school is one of the biggest in the country.

Multi-day learn-to-ski packages lure new skiers into the fold, and there are now programs aimed at advanced skiers too (Workshops in Racing and Bump Skiing, five-day Mountain Ski Weeks, Learn to Be A Ski Instructor Weeks, Superstars for children, and the like). Thus Killington has remained not only the place to ski but also the place for good skiers to become better ones.

Smith has made his ski area the dominant ski resort in the East. It ranks with Vail and Mammoth Mountain, California, in annual skier visits. And in 1976, Killington bought Mount Snow, a popular medium-size mountain an hour to the south. On any given winter day, one-third of all the skiers in Vermont are likely to be at one of these two mountains, now under the umbrella of SKI Limited. In 1988 it bought Goldmine in Southern California, launching an assault on the west coast market.

SKIING

With six fully interconnected lift-and-trail networks, Killington is like half a dozen smaller ski areas rolled into one. There are two main ways to get into the trail system. The traditional one is via the five-mile access road to one of three parking lots—Snowshed to the left, Killington straight ahead, and Rams Head to the right. Newer access points are off Route 4, the main east-west conduit through the middle of Vermont. There are huge parking lots at the bottom of the Northeast Passage triple chair to Sunrise Mountain and the gondola. Another access road leads from the highway to the Bear Mountain base, with one high-speed quad chairlift and two doubles and an intimidating view of bruising bumps. If Bear Mountain were the first thing unwary skiers saw, all but the most stalwart would drive right past Killington.

The ski area has cut and graded its terrain so that even novices may ski the easiest runs on each of the six mountains as early as their third day on skis. There is a wealth of novice turf from which to choose. Killington's terrain is so complex that the area offers free, daily, meet-the-mountain tours for all skiing levels. Many regulars have staked out their favorite quadrant of the trail map and ski it again and again. The poster-size trail map is a marvel of cartography. The terrain is shown three ways: topographically, showing elevation; schematically, with trails color-coded by difficulty; and aerially, from a vantage point that shows how the peaks lie in relation to one another.

Killington Peak is for traditional New England skiers, who like their terrain steep and narrow. They just don't come much hairier than Cascade, Escapade, Downdraft, or Flume, the last a knee-rocking, rock-hopping liftline run under the old Killington double chair. This peak is also for early-season enthusiasts and late-season die-hards, for it's here that the Glade's triple chair serves the runs where snow is made early, blown deep, and stockpiled. Rams Head, with just one old double chairlift and seven trails, is the smallest, most intimate of Killington's networks. But in a world of high-volume cafeteria production lines and high-speed lifts, Rams Head has a traditional feeling and usually fewer crowds. Snowdon, a peak between Killington and Rams Head, offers a near-even mix of novice, intermediate, and advanced runs.

Killington's sexiest terrain is on the three newer peaks—Skye, Bear, and Sunshine—served by the Superstar quad, a high-speed detachable chair added for 1987-88 to provide quick access from the Killington base. Skye Peak (the oldest of the new sectors) is basically easy skiing, serving as the pivotal point between old Killington trails and newer ones. When the four-passenger gondola was built a decade earlier, some people thought it was foolish to put in so long a lift to serve such mild terrain as Juggernaut and Great Eastern, two of the longest, flattest runs in skidom. But Killington knew that a gondola along the highway would be a year-round cash cow—reaping a healthy summer and fall crop of sightseers' dollars. Cindy Nelson, who used to train at Killington with her U.S. Ski Team mates, called Juggernaut, with its yawn-provoking 6 percent pitch, the "Audubon special," claiming that you could ski the whole ten miles in a tuck and still be able to watch the birds in the woods. As if to certify her opinion, Killington now runs a race called the Juggernaut Alpine/Cross-Country Derby, in which two-racer teams of one Alpine and one cross-country skier tuck, glide, skate, and pole down the 54,695-foot course.

Should you make a turn onto Frost Line, however, a tame cutover to Bear Mountain, you'll wake up fast. Bear drops like a canyon wall off the end of a ridge, offering skiing so steep and so stupendously moguled that it simply has no peers in New England. There are three main super-steep runs, but each is as wide as three conventional trails. Devil's Fiddle and Wildfire are like parentheses bracketing the Bear Mountain terrain. Down the middle, like an exclamation point that really means it, is Outer Limits, the longest, steepest, and most consistent ski slope in New England. Calculating a 2,808-foot length and a 1,216-foot vertical equals an awesome average gradient of 48 percent. Ski it once, especially in spring when it is so mogully that it looks like a parking lot for snow-covered Volkswagen Beetles, and Fiddle and Wildfire suddenly seem tame. Ski it three times, and your legs will probably have turned to Jell-O. Ski it well, and consider entering the annual Bear Mountain Mogul Challenge.

Sunrise Mountain is Killington's easternmost terrain. There are a couple of steeps down near the bottom of the Northeast Passage chair, but everything else is solid green—and so it should be, because these runs essentially serve the growing condominium and second-home community called Sunrise Village, a classy complex that has gone a long way toward upgrading the whole Killington experience.

LODGING

A criticism of Killington has been that it has had no definable village center, minimal slopeside lodging, and little atmosphere. Those craving close-in accommodations had a choice of the Mountain Inn and a handful of early condominiums on the lee side of the Snowshed parking lot. Those who wanted a village went to Plymouth Union, a nearby hamlet most famous for being the home of Calvin Coolidge. Those who sought charm drove half-an-hour to Woodstock, an upscale New England town that virtually oozes with white-clapboard, apple-butter ambiance. Now the most visible accommodations to the casual visitor are more than a dozen lodges and motels on the access road leading to Killington and strung along Route 4. On the access road are such medium-priced standards as the Red Rob Inn, the Killington Village Inn, skiers' traditional MAP lodges, and the Chalet Killington and North Star Lodge. Notable B&Bs include the Chalet Salzburg, cozily Austrian in feeling, and the well-appointed Chalet Killington. All offer convenience to the mountain and most offer skier-pleasing amenities as well. Two of the best along Route 4 are the Cortina Inn, a post modern hotel with an excellent restaurant, and the classic Long Trail Lodge, atop Sherburne Pass, a favorite of hikers before the ski boom began. The Turn of River Lodge is a cozy, old-style place near the gondola base; it is ideal for budget watchers. A bit farther afield are such charmers as the Salt Ash Inn in Plymouth, a white frame beauty built as a stagecoach stop in 1830; the Brandon Inn in Brandon, built thirty-five years earlier (and recently refurbished with great style); and the Mountaintop Inn in Chittenden, a spectacular, isolated resort. Mountaintop and the Woodstock Inn in Woodstock also have their own outstanding cross-country trail systems and touring programs.

APRÈS-SKI AND RESTAURANTS

Since much of Killington's business ranges from college groups to high-living, hard-playing urban swingles, après-ski has always been a big part of the scene. It starts with a quick beer at the Snowshed or Killington base lodge, or perhaps a stop at the Red Rob, the Grey Bonnet, or Charity's, where live music is featured. Then the action shifts into high gear at the Wobbly Barn and the Pickel Barrel, two loud, late-night landmarks.

Fine dining came late to the Killington area, but there is now a choice of excellent places purveying warmth, charm, and fine fare. Annabelle's and Hemingway's are historic houses, elegantly redone and serving continental cuisine. Countryman's Pleasure and Casa Blanca also do continental, while Churchill's, the Grist Mill, and Royal Hearthside specialize in New England dishes like hearty chowders, fine seafood, and classic pie and pudding desserts. For more informal fare, Marge & John's serves all-day stick-to-the-ribs breakfasts, and Annabelle's Tavern, Cafe Killington, and Mother Shapiro's are good bets for moderately priced, casual dining.

Survey a hundred Vermont skiers, and few will claim that Killington is the resort they love the most, but it is the place knowledgeable skiers have come to respect the most. People ski there by the thousands, initially because they are attracted by the outstanding learn-to-ski programs and good deals on multi-day stays at Killington. Later, as they compare it with other places, they discover that Killington does have it all: huge terrain, the most reliable conditions, skiing for all ability levels, accommodations and restaurants of all styles and for all pocketbooks, and reasonable accessibility even for a weekend. There are crowds on the mountain, but the area does its best to disperse them among all those lodges, lifts, and trails. With no traditional village center, the ski area and all the services that have grown up around it have gone the extra mile to put together easy-to-book packages for skiers of all levels and to offer what has to be the most informative library of clear, concise information brochures in skidom.

Lake Tahoe, California/Nevada

THE LAKE TAHOE BASIN HAS
THE LARGEST, DENSEST
CONCENTRATION OF SKI
AREAS IN AMERICA

Austria has its Arlberg. France has its Three Valleys. Italy has its Super Dolomiti. And the United States has the Lake Tahoe basin, the largest, densest concentration of ski areas in the land. Some twenty cluster around the twenty-two-mile-long lake, mostly on the California side. But the five largest, which offer a joint lift pass, are the ones that make this area a worthy destination. The ruggedly scenic high Sierra range not only has some of the best bowl skiing in North America, but it also is buried by snowstorms whose dumps are measured in feet rather than inches. The ski season normally stretches from early November until May.

Skiers divide the lake into the North Shore, where Alpine Meadows, Squaw Valley, and Northstar-at-Tahoe are located, and the South Shore where Heavenly Valley and Kirkwood are located. Après-skiers divide the lake into Nevada, where there is twenty-four-hour nightlife and legalized gambling, and California, where the action is much more sedate.

Decades before there was a rope tow at Shawbridge, Quebec, or Woodstock, Vermont, before there was a chairlift at Stowe or Sun Valley, before there was a tram at Cannon Mountain or even in Europe, there was skiing in the Sierra. Skiing came to America with a Norwegian immigrant named John A. "Snowshoe" Thomson. Infected with gold fever, living in relative isolation, he was struck by the absence of winter contact between the mining camps on the eastern and western slopes of the Sierra. In 1856, he felled an oak tree, carved a pair of twenty-five-pound skis, and began hauling mail across ninety mountainous miles between Genoa, Nevada, and Placerville, California. Until replaced by the railroad in 1872, Thomson was the only winter overland link between Northern California and the rest of the country.

Some other mid-nineteenth century miners were less interested in work than play. Rowdy gold miners began to lash long skis to their boots and race straight down the mountainsides at up to eighty miles an hour in pursuit of entertainment, prize money, and glory. Such events were probably the first professional ski competitions. In 1913, an old mining lift began hauling skiers uphill in Truckee, today the site of the Boreal ski area. The ski tradition started by Thomson has never died out in the Sierra.

"Tahoe: Land of Contrasts" aptly describes the contemporary Tahoe ski scene. You can stay at an old frame lodge in an ancient mining town, a slopeside condo with a private Jacuzzi, or a high-rise casino-hotel in Reno. You can ski Northstar where all runs are easy or Squaw Valley where hardly any are. You can even ski between California and Nevada without removing your skis, because Heavenly Valley is bisected by the state line. You can ski till you drop, gamble till you're broke, or simply stare at the mesmerizing blue of the lake—one of the most scenic centerpieces in all of skiing.

SQUAW VALLEY

Whatever you do, though, you must ski Squaw Valley. A century after Snowshoe Thomson introduced skiing to the new world, Squaw Valley brought skiing into the modern era when it hosted the 1960 Winter Olympics. Squaw Valley is where America's Penny Pitou and Betsy Snite snared all three silver medals in women's Alpine skiing, where Carol Heiss and Hayes Alan Jenkins enchanted the world with their gold-medal figure skating, and where the Americans walloped the Russians in hockey to win a gold—a feat they did not repeat until Lake Placid twenty years later.

Squaw Valley offers the best skiing in California.

Squaw Valley was the creation of a trio of fanatical skiers: Martin Arrouge, son of a local Basque sheep rancher, found the terrain; Wayne Poulsen, son of a Reno optician, assembled the land; and Alex Cushing, a Harvard-educated Boston Brahmin, raised the money to build a ski area there. When Squaw Valley opened on Thanksgiving weekend in 1949, there was one chairlift (then the world's longest), two rope tows, and a fifty-bed lodge.

Expansion was marked by mishaps—three avalanches in five years uprooted lift towers, floods twice inundated the lodge, and fire once leveled it. But Squaw Valley, undeterred by disaster, won the bidding for the 1960 Winter Olympics, beating out Reno, Sun Valley, and Innsbruck, Austria. They were the first televised Olympics and put Squaw Valley on the map.

SKIING

Squaw's formidable amphitheater of mountainous terrain quite simply provides the best skiing in California. In the manner of the Alps, a 150-passenger tram and a swift six-passenger gondola whisk skiers to two wide plateaus, High Camp and Gold Coast respectively. From there, a dozen chairlifts—doubles, triples, and quads—climb to three peaks. There is a peerless assortment of wide trails, awesome treeless bowls, and nasty chutes. When the great dealer in the sky was passing out ski terrain, Squaw Valley received a full house.

From the base the highest skiable point in sight is Squaw Peak, topping out at 8,900 feet. Featuring couloirs barely wider than a ski length and shimmering snowfields bristling with big bumps, this is where the hotshots congregate. Emigrant Peak, a bit lower, features long gentle cruising runs and ski-to access to the area that is tucked behind it, the Shirley Lake/Granite Chief sector, which rises to 9,200 feet. Though hidden from Squaw's hub, this section, offering intermediate and advanced trails, has become one of the most popular. From this area it is possible to ski back to the base—and some good skiers do. The homeward runs are gorgeous and demanding: long, steep ravines and surprising glades of tall firs, with lifts sailing overhead and sculptured red rocks on each side. But most skiers, having fried their thighs, are happy to ride down.

When Wayne and Sandy Poulsen were scouting Squaw Valley in the deep, heavy snow that is referred to as Sierra cement, Sandy named a rugged slope hanging over the valley KT-22 because she had to do twenty-two kick turns before she got to the bottom. Out of the tram/gondola orbit and away from the glitzy mid-mountain facilities, KT-22 is a haven for experts. Relentlessly steep, startlingly moguled, and made even more difficult because there is no true bail-out (Chicken Bowl, allegedly the easy way down, isn't), KT-22 is an ultimate experience.

LODGING

Over the years, Olympic Valley, the base village, has been greatly improved. There is now a pleasant mall, and both the Olympic Village Inn and the Squaw Valley Inn offer modern accommodations. Other skiers overnight in Tahoe City or Truckee.

The steeps of Wolverine Bowl at Alpine Meadows.

ALPINE MEADOWS

Squaw Valley's nearest neighbor, Alpine Meadows, is also a multi-peaked ski area, offering a grand range of terrain on a 1,797-foot vertical. But its pace is less frenetic and high-powered than Squaw's. Alpine has long labored under the inaccurate reputation of being an easy mountain. Six great bowls, 100 trails, and 2,000 acres of skiing, including ungroomed steeps with a distinct out-of-bounds flavor, do not make an easy mountain.

SKIING

Alpine's lifts rise to three peaks. The Summit chair to Ward Peak provides 1,555 vertical feet of demanding terrain, dropping from a razorback ridge into the bowl of choice: Wolverine for super steeps, or Beaver for trees mixed with steeps.

*The average snowfall in the
Lake Tahoe area is among
the highest in America.*

The Roundhouse chair connects the base with a mostly intermediate hump that pokes up in
the middle of the ski area like a big dumpling sitting in a soup bowl. It also provides access via
the Alpine chair to Ward Peak, which leads to another bowl as well as to dizzying, double-diamond
couloirs like Counterweight Gully, Our Father, and Palisades. A short climb and a traverse over
the side of Ward Peak lead to the Sherwood Bowl, which boasts splendid powder skiing when
there is new snow, grand spring skiing when there is corn, and just plain fun cruising the rest
of the time.

Alpine's third mountain is Scott's, a densely treed hummock that seems anomalous in the Tahoe
world of open bowls and wide runs. The front of Scott's is a crazy rockscape of escarpments and
cliffs punctuated by gnarled trees and occasional ribbons of skiable snow, somehow woven into
a web of black-diamond routes. Scott's backside offers wide blue-square runs for joyful medium-
level skiing. Alpine Meadows has first-rate day lodges with comfortable sundecks and well-equipped
barbecue stations.

LODGING AND APRÈS-SKI

River Ranch, a rustic lodge beside the Truckee River, is the closest recommended accommodation. Otherwise, Alpine and Squaw skiers tend to stay in Truckee or at lakeside motels or condominium developments in Tahoe City along the northwestern shore. Hacienda del Sol and Rosie's on the lake and the Passage in Truckee are good après-ski and dining choices. In Tahoe City, the finest dining is at Christy Hill, Sunnyside (also a B&B), and Wolfdale's.

NORTHSTAR-AT-TAHOE

Northstar-at-Tahoe is a congenial family resort. The condominiums at the bottom of the mountain comprise a stylish village nestled in the trees. There is a small shopping mall and a spacious, gracious day lodge. The 2,200-foot vertical is nothing to sneeze at, though the skiing, most of which is reached via shuttle gondola, is mostly easy—and all pleasant. It is ideal for new skiers, for take-it-easy types, or for advanced skiers whose egos, bruised from Squaw or Alpine, can use some boosting. Wide super-cruisers predominate. The front of the mountain actually is folded into two-and-a-half (arguably three) faces with elegant boulevards cut through the trees. The Ironhorse chair on the backside has the steepest terrain. Occasionally, one or two trails—usually Rapids—are allowed to mogul up under the chairlift.

HEAVENLY VALLEY

The giant of the South Shore is Heavenly Valley, a contender for the honor of being America's biggest ski area—"biggest" depending on what one measures. Heavenly is a twenty-square-mile behemoth spilling across nine peaks in two states. In the East, a 2,000-foot vertical is the dividing line between large areas and all others. In the Rockies, it's 3,000. Heavenly has a 3,600-vertical on the California side and 2,700 in Nevada. The lift census boggles the mind: a fifty-passenger aerial tram, six triple chairs, ten doubles, and five surface lifts. Heavenly, which has had more snowmaking than all other Tahoe areas combined, is also expanding its system into one of the world's largest. And, from the California side, where snow-capped mountains meet the iridescent waters of the lake, Heavenly has one of the best views of any ski area in captivity.

SKIING

Peculiar geography situates the main port of entry for skiers on the California side. Three large lifts—the tram and a couple of chairs—shoot straight up the mountain. Beneath them are steep bump runs that shoot straight down. One, Gunbarrel, is a bumper of such meanness that sadistic spectators sit in the huge base lodge to witness what havoc can be wrought on skiers who try to show off but shouldn't.

These lifts unload on the first of the peaks, gateway to a splendid assortment of what are called novice and intermediate runs. Generously cut through the woods, this terrain is made for long GS turns. Still, sweet skiing can become more challenging when the altitude makes you feel light-headed, when the clouds move in to erase the line between snow and sky, when new snow gums up, when the moguls build to terrifying heights, or when any combination of the above exists.

The Sky chair, leading to the Nevada side, is less crowded. On this side, most of the standard-looking trails are marked, but if you're looking for expert runs, it pays to ski with someone who knows his way around. There's Milky Way Bowl, for instance, a great U-shaped trough that tickles the toes and tingles the spine. It's on the map, but a devil to find unless you know where to leave the catwalk, which trees to squeeze past, and where to traverse along the side of an unspeakably steep canyon wall. Or there is Mott Canyon, a precipitous, unmarked glade that drops off the side of the mountain. It's a thousand feet of stupendous tree skiing. At the bottom, a snowcat is stationed to haul skiers back out because there are no lifts.

On the Nevada side, there are two base lodges. On the California side, there is one day lodge at the base, one at the upper terminal of the tram, and one tucked into a hollow near the Sky and Canyon chairs. On-the-mountain barbecuing is the order of the day. You can buy a raw meat pattie, a roll, and some condiments at a glowing charcoal brazier, and grill your own.

LODGING

The strip in Stateline and its more subdued continuation in South Lake Tahoe offer the greatest concentration of accommodations. For some, the contrast of skiing while staying in a year-round lakeside lodge or, even more dramatically, at a casino-hotel, is appealing. Others prefer more ski-oriented accommodations. Tahoe Seasons, within walking distance of the tram, is a modern luxury hotel. Equally convenient are the Sitzmark, Summit, and Concept Sierra condos. On the Nevada side, Ridge Tahoe is a posh complex near the base of the Stagecoach chair. Eagle's Nest Inn is truly slopeside, while Heavenly North Condos, Tahoe Lakeview, and Tahoe Ridge Sierra are condos near the parking lot, and the Ridgeview Hotel is just down the road.

KIRKWOOD

Like Northstar, Kirkwood has a beautiful day lodge and on-site condominiums. Like Alpine Meadows, its 2,000 acres of skiing include steep mogul chutes that drop one after another off a long ridge. And like Squaw Valley, it has a couple of splendiferous bowls. It shares with the rest of the big Tahoe ski areas the geography which accommodates skiing on several faces. In addition to the admirable advanced terrain, Kirkwood has some of the best ultra-gentle beginner runs of any of the major Sierra areas. For some inexplicable reason, though, Kirkwood is considered a small ski area—an erroneous notion if ever there was one.

The two major chairs open up to a fine assortment of devilish cornices, hanging walls, an exuberance of bump runs. The long base-to-summit Cornice chair leads to terrain that r a point-of-entry leap off the edge to one of the many maxi-mogul routes down a choice Wagon Wheel is the official name of the next-longest chair, but skiers have referred Wall for so long, that management put both names on the trail map. The Wall run chillingly steep, unforgiving in length, and sprouting as many moguls as there are s Sierra night sky. The Wall makes the runs off the Cornice chair seem mild. bowls high above the trees elevate Kirkwood beyond its reputation.

The Sunrise chair, on another face of Kirkwood's wrap-around *massif*, unfolds a gentler bowl—one whose routes are tagged with blue not black and one which, as its name implies, is at its best when kissed with the morning light. Many of these runs funnel into the trees—sometimes settling into broad boulevards, sometimes fanning into tree skiing, sometimes requiring a detour around a sudden cliff.

Tahoe is one of the greatest ski areas in the United States, combining casino country, where hotels and restaurants operate as loss leaders for the gambling industry, with skiing that offers an almost unparalleled variety of fun and challenge.

Park City, Deer Valley & ParkWest, Utah

THE THREE AREAS, WHICH MAKE UP
THE LARGEST MEGA-RESORT IN
UTAH, ALL OFFER TERRIFIC SKIING,
BUT THEIR INDIVIDUAL STYLES ARE
VASTLY DIFFERENT, RANGING FROM
FUNKY AND CASUAL TO ELEGANT

Park City is a tremendous ski area that is by many measures the biggest in Utah. The town's Main Street, lined with attractively spruced-up nineteenth-century storefronts, is designated a National Historic District. Surrounding the shopping street are all manner of lodgings where 10,000 skiers can be comfortably housed. There are inexpensive motels and ski dorms, exquisite bed-and-breakfast inns, posh slopeside condos, and full-service resort complexes with their tennis courts, health clubs, and other contemporary amenities. Swimming pools, hot tubs, and saunas abound for guests of all but the most economical accommodations. The community also boasts more than fifty restaurants, a comparable number of shops, and a mind-bending array of non-ski and après-ski options.

The Park City ski area, built on Treasure Mountain, which yielded $400 million worth of silver before the mines were closed, weighs in with eighty-two trails cut through lush stands of aspen and spruce, and 650 acres of bowl skiing. The 3,100-foot vertical drop is equal to Snowbird's, and the lift capacity of nearly 19,000 skiers an hour dwarfs anything else in the state. Add the considerable attributes of its near neighbors, swank Deer Valley and laid-back ParkWest, and it's clear that the town of Park City is the heavyweight champion of Utah skiing.

This resort town is located near the end of Parley's Canyon, an easy hour's drive from Salt Lake City International Airport. Parley's is really more of a broad valley than a typical steep-walled Utah canyon, offering space for facilities such as golf courses, ski-touring trails, and sites for launching hot-air balloons.

The three areas all offer terrific skiing, but their individual styles are vastly different. Deer Valley is a Mercedes, all luxury and comfort. Park City is a Ford, serviceable and flexible. And ParkWest is a VW Beetle, basic and frill-free.

Park City is *Jederman's* ski area, an egalitarian place where actors David and Meredith Baxter Birney, who have a home nearby, may stand in line behind a family from Phoenix or a couple from Columbus—or ahead of some stars from the U.S. Ski Team, which headquarters there. Attire ranges from rhinestone-belted Bogners to travel-worn team parkas. At Deer Valley, the runs are groomed to putting-green smoothness, and the skiers, regardless of how well they do or don't ski, are dressed in haute-chic. ParkWest has a casual atmosphere and minimal crowds, except on Saturdays when hordes of Salt Lake City locals appear, clad in CB and other practical, long-wearing ski clothes.

This trio—plus Brighton and Solitude in Big Cottonwood Canyon and Alta and Snowbird in Little Cottonwood—are skiable via one interchangeable coupon book. Park City is also the gateway to the five-area Utah Interconnect, a guided out-of-bounds excursion for competent, confident skiers that starts at the top of Jupiter Bowl, continues through the Cottonwoods, and finishes at Snowbird. The Interconnect is a preview of what will probably be America's largest ski complex, for the likelihood of future lifts linking these three adjacent canyons is real. The Cottonwoods, however, are narrow, with no possibility of supporting large developments, so Park City is now and is likely to remain the mega-resort of Utah's Wasatch Range.

PARK CITY

The Park City ski area is, in many ways, an all-American place whose terrain, a balanced mix of wide slopes, traditional trails, and open bowls, exemplifies the cumulative theories of American ski-area layout. The red, white, and blue logo of the U.S. Ski Team is prominently, proudly, and patriotically displayed, yet Park City is international too. It has a sister city program with Courchevel, a fashionable resort in the French Alps, and it has hosted the opening races of the World Cup, a season-long series which to European ski fans is like the World Series and the Triple Crown all rolled into one.

There are two access points to the Park City ski area. The Town Lift, a triple chair built in 1985, loads just below Main Street, uniting town and mountain. The Resort Center, an attractive contemporary brick plaza of shops, restaurants, and condominiums, is the main base area. Park City's four-passenger gondola cars that leave from the Resort Center are painted with primary red, blue, and yellow, colors that contrast with the white snow and, frequently, azure sky. But this two-and-a-half-mile lift, while still the longest gondola in the West, is really a low-capacity dinosaur, better for sightseeing than efficient uphill transportation.

Skiers intent on avoiding the inevitably long gondola lines use a series of chairlifts to get to the top, which is 9,400 feet above sea level. There one finds the Summit House, a popular mountaintop restaurant. From the top, novices comfortably ski the broad Claimjumper, which, like so many other mountain features, owes its name to Park City's mining past. Intermediates can sail down nearly a score of blue-square runs that drop 1,200 vertical feet off the sides of the ridges toward Thaynes Canyon. Bump skiers head for the steep precincts of The Hoist, Double Jack, or the run that goes directly under the Thaynes chair. These runs alone are enough to make Park City a big-league ski area, but it is the high bowls soaring behind the main mountain which catch the lightest powder and which are of highest quality.

The Jupiter chair, which ups Park City's total vertical by another six hundred feet, ferries skiers to the 10,000-foot elevation, past spikey evergreens that are a rugged contrast to the gentler trees lining the lower trails. Jupiter Bowl is a broad, steep cirque where powder skiers dance through

In Deer Valley the luxurious Stein Eriksen Lodge maintains high standards of quality and service.

the trees. Purists climb over Pioneer Ridge to ski Puma Bowl and McConkey's Bowl or over Shadow Ridge into Scott's Bowl. Eventually, Puma and McConkey's will have a lift, but Scott's is to remain accessible only to those willing to hike in.

DEER VALLEY

Hiking would be anathema to Deer Valley skiers, a group so pampered that the unremitting fulfillment of their greatest expectations has created a new level of ski-resort service. Deer Valley does everything but ski for its guests. Uniformed attendants remove skis from roof racks and guard them until arriving skiers have parked their cars. (Why carry skis across a parking lot?) A complimentary basket check in the Snow Park Lodge frees this elegant base facility from the unsightly melange of after-ski boots and tote bags, and the complimentary ski corrals outside Snow Park and the mid-mountain Silver Lake Lodge provide security for ski equipment. If you've shelled out up to $1,600 for a pair of Pure Gold skis, you certainly wouldn't want anyone walking off with them. The suntans displayed on the lounge chairs at McHenry's Beach, the sunny terrace beside

*Olympic champion Stein Eriksen
is director of skiing at Deer Valley.*

Silver Lake Lodge, might have been started at Palm Springs or Palm Beach, Mustique or Majorca.

Doesn't that glamorous woman, her face obscured by giant sunglasses, look familiar? Cybil Shepard? Or Victoria Principal? Or Jane Fonda? They've all skied Deer Valley, as have Steve Garvey, Hal Linden, Roger Penske, and two Bruces—Willis and Springsteen. The Boss even learned to ski at Deer Valley, and Fonda has a condo there.

The faucets in the restrooms are gold, and the metal of the lift chairs is anodized in a gold tone, too. The chairlift pads are basic black but feel double-thick. During a storm, no flake of snow escapes the brush before a courteous lift attendant slides each chair under the posteriors of Deer Valley skiers as deftly as they might be seated at dinner by the maitre d' at Phillipe's, in Deer Valley's new Stag Lodge.

Tame novice runs, undulating intermediate cruisers and respectable steeps stretch over the two mountains, Bald Eagle and Bald Mountain, which are separated by a saddle where Silver Lake Lodge nestles. The runs are more than merely groomed; they are *manicured*. It was only at the behest of some of Deer Valley's better skiers—including Director of Skiing Stein Eriksen, the ageless Olympic champion who runs a luxurious slopeside lodge bearing his name—that the ski area was persuaded to groom a little less. Now some of the black-diamond runs off the Sultan chair, the area's most recent addition, are permitted to mogul up and provide a level of challenge previously unavailable at Deer Valley.

PARKWEST

Just the opposite grooming policy is in effect at ParkWest, a favorite haunt of powder-hungry Salt Lake City skiers. ParkWest is skiing as it used to be. There are so few lines that there's no need for lift mazes, and so little skier traffic spread over forty-six trails that the powder lingers. The area's singular friendliness comes not only from a management policy to hire cheerful, smiling extroverts but also because ParkWest skiers all know one another—as well as all the area employees. ParkWest is ham on rye—a lively area where the pink flamingos staked out beside Soup's On, the A-frame at the bottom of the Ironhorse lift, don't seem a plastic feather out of place.

There is a wide beginner slope at the base of the mountain, but ParkWest's potent lure for Salt Lake *cognoscenti* is in the powder chutes off the Ironhorse chair and the tree skiing on a steep face off the Arrowhead chair.

APRÈS-SKI AND RESTAURANTS

The choices of skiing around the Park City resort community are mirrored in the variety and vitality of its après-ski life. The stores on Main Street, which once carried groceries, hardware, and clothing have metamorphosed into restaurants, more restaurants, still more restaurants, galleries, and boutiques. There is a new indoor shopping mall, its Main Street face in keeping with historic-district requirements but its interior aglitter with temptations. Park City is even a corporate headquarters of sorts. It is the international home of Mrs. Field's Cookies; and it is the headquarters (and main and only plant) of the Schirf Brewing Company, founded in 1986 to produce Wasatch Ale and Wasatch Gold, a lighter beer.

Immediately after skiing, the action moves to the Resort Center, where oceans of brew—Wasatch and others—are consumed by legions of thirsty skiers. At night, the choice is between dining and entertainment at the Resort Center or on Main Street. Will it be steak at the Claimjumper or tacos at the Irish Camel? Italian-style veal at Mileti's or Swiss-style veal at Adolph's? The lavish seafood buffet up at Deer Valley or charbroiled baby back ribs at The Eating Establishment?

Getting a drink—before, with, or after dinner—involves one of several transparent ruses to circumvent Utah's bizarre liquor laws. Beer is served over the counter, as in other states, but wine and hard stuff must either be purchased by the drink in a "private club" which visitors may "join" for a nominal sum or bought by the bottle from an on- or off-premises liquor store and consumed with "setups" (ice, mixers, or simply glasses) brought by the waiter or waitress. The requisite circumnavigation of conventional drinking hasn't cut consumption any, nor has it silenced the music which is such a vital component of the after-ski scene.

LODGING

Park City has lodging for every taste and budget. For convenience plus luxury, a Resort Center or Shadow Ridge condo can't be beat. For atmosphere, there is an unusually fine choice of charming bed-and-breakfast inns. Guests can ski right to the sauna behind the cozy and casual Old Miner's Lodge. Nearby is the landmark Washington School Inn. The most unusual is Snowed Inn between Park City and ParkWest. Looking for all the world like a Victorian jewel, this antique-filled reproduction was, in fact, built in 1986, combining the visual appeal of the last century with the creature comforts of this one.

Park City/Deer Valley/ParkWest (along with Alta and Snowbird) are perhaps the most accessible ski resorts in the country. They not only provide matchless day-skiing but they are literally only a cab ride from the airport. Businessmen on a trip from New York to Los Angeles can and do book a stopover in Salt Lake. Packing only their ski clothes and renting their equipment, they can enjoy a mini-ski vacation without missing a beat. The Park City cluster also benefits from the consistently deep powder snowfall for which the Wasatch Range is famous. And finally this complex offers an extraordinary variety of skiing, services, après-ski activity, lodging, and dining.

Ski 93, New Hampshire

SKI 93 ENCOMPASSES BEGINNER
HILLS AND STEEP, RUGGED
DESCENTS, HEALTH CLUBS,
COUNTRY INNS, AND BEAUTIFUL
NEW ENGLAND VILLAGES

Cannon Mountain, Loon Mountain, Waterville Valley, and the smaller ski areas flanking Interstate 93, the Granite State's main north-south highway, combine into one mega-destination featuring joint lift privileges. Within about thirty miles are the interstate exits for Tenney Mountain, a small family ski area, and Cannon Mountain, a challenging New England classic in Franconia Notch. Between them are the exits for the built-for-skiing resorts of Loon and Waterville, and a few miles farther is Bretton Woods, in the shadow of Mount Washington, equally attractive to downhill and cross-country aficionados.

It is impossible to talk about American skiing without mentioning Franconia, an archetypically quaint New England hamlet where various elements of American ski tradition took root. The largely self-taught skiers of the 1920s hiked up hills and skied down, using any method that worked to steer and stop. In 1929, Katherine Peckett, daughter of the owner of Peckett's-on-Sugar-Hill, a summer resort near Franconia, returned from a ski vacation in St. Anton, Austria, raving about Hannes Schneider and his Arlberg Ski School. Peckett's had long welcomed a handful of off-season guests who came to play in the snow, but Katherine foresaw the potential of skiing in America. She recruited four Austrian instructors.

The first was Sig Buchmayr, an all-around skier then on the stunt ski-jumping circuit. He was soon joined by Kurt Thalheimer, Harold Paumgarten, and Richard Suiter. They constituted the first ski school in the United States. This generation of instructors, who taught Schneider's innovative by-the-book progression of turns, inspired the students' imitative phrase, "Bend ze knees, two dollars, please." Wearing floppy pants, wool socks, bulky jackets, and peaked caps—and outfitted with clunky leather boots and long wooden skis—scores of tyros learned the rudiments of snowplow and stem turns. They later graduated to stem christies, a remarkable accomplishment on the ungroomed meadow beside the hotel.

CANNON MOUNTAIN

At the same time, a group of sporty Boston businessmen formed the Hochgebirge Ski Club, and in 1930 they challenged the young jocks of the Dartmouth Outing Club to a ski race. That first invitational downhill, following a walk-up, was held on an old carriage road on Mount Moosilauke near Dartmouth College. In 1932, under the auspices of the Franconia Ski Club (which Katherine Peckett also had a hand in forming), the Civilian Conservation Corps cut the Taft Racing Trail, the first in America, on Cannon Mountain, a 4,146-foot granite peak in Franconia State Park. The Taft was only eight feet wide, and before racers could ski it, they had to strap sealskins to the bottoms of their skis and climb it.

In 1933, the Hochgebirge Challenge Cup was moved to the Taft, and Cannon Mountain became the center of skiing in the East. Alexander Bright—a Boston stockbroker, a "Hochie," and a racer who had skied in Europe, came up with the idea of constructing an Alpine-style aerial tram on Cannon, which could be used by skiers in winter and sightseers in summer. Bright and his Hochie allies needed three years to convince the state to fund the tram, but in 1938, "Cannon I" sailed its maiden voyage up this compelling peak and into the history books. It was America's first cable car—and for two decades the only ride to the summit. The tram cost $250,000 and carried twenty-four skiers (or twenty-seven summer sightseers) for sixty cents a ride. This early lift-served ski area—a concept which still had no name—included five rugged trails averaging two miles in length. Of the original quintet, Ravine and Cannon are still skied, while Coppermine and Tucker Brook have been abandoned. Old Taft is still shown as a ghost trail on the area map and is also memorialized with its namesake, the Taft Race Course, where a modern version of the Hochgebirge Challenge is still run. Hardscrabble was cut two years later, the last new trail before World War II, and it too is still in use—steep, twisting, and appropriately named. Forty-two years and nearly 6.6-million passengers after it was built, Cannon I was replaced in 1980 with a faster, three-times-larger, $4.3-million tram.

Skiers and skiing have changed since the days of Katherine Peckett, Sig Buchmayr, and Alexander Bright, but the indomitability that characterized Cannon and its skiers from the earliest days remains. Today Cannon is the site of the New England Ski Museum, which displays a Cannon I tram car, old photographs, memorabilia, and artifacts from those bygone days. Cannon is one of two state-owned-and-run ski areas in New Hampshire (the other is Mount Sunapee far to the south), and the legislature maintains a tight hold on the area's purse strings. Consequently, Cannon still has such anomalies as a pair of parallel T-bars serving the summit trails and a main lift that is not near the main trails! Because summer tourism was a high priority, the tram rises over unskiable rock cliffs, while the runs go down the other side. Chairlifts now serve the lower mountain, enabling skiers to get from the bottom to the top without the tram. Otherwise, it's necessary to ski the steep connector trails—Avalanche, Paulie's Folly, Rocket, and Zoomer—to get back to the tram base.

Those lower chairlifts also serve the Peabody Slopes, a half-dozen runs, novice and intermediate by Cannon standards. The main runs on Cannon fall into three categories: difficult, more difficult, and most difficult. In part, the challenge comes from the rugged terrain itself. Even with snowmaking and grooming, which came later to Cannon than to other big mountains in the state, the upper mountain remains windblown, icy, and hardscrabbly.

The layout, in which no ski trails cross the tramline, leaves Cannon with two base areas. The modest tram and Peabody base lodges are both bursting on those wonderful weekends and holidays when *la toute* Boston seems to be skiing. During most weekdays, however, there's excess capacity. Still it remains a place for the dedicated, for the purists, for those who want to pit themselves against the strongest challenges New England terrain and weather can unleash.

LODGING

Franconia is the lodging choice for skiers who wish to ski Cannon and also to steep themselves in New England tradition. Lovett's Inn by Lafayette Brook, built in 1784, is within sight of Cannon. It is lovingly tended by Charles Lovett, Jr., son of one of the mountain's pioneers. If Cannon is what skiing used to be, Lovett's is what a ski lodge ought to be—an antique-filled inn of incredible warmth where fine food and a bit of formality are still to be found. Nearly as ancient is the Sugar Hill Inn, a 1789 farmhouse that is now a quaint ten-room inn. The Rivagale Inn in Franconia has just a handful of rooms, but its spacious lounge offers some of the best après-ski in what is otherwise a quiet corner of the White Mountains. The Horse & Hound is a small traditional lodge of exceptional charm. The Franconia Inn, located on 117 rustic acres, is the largest of the inns and, with such amenities as a hot tub and a pleasant rathskeller, the most lavishly equipped. All have commendable dining rooms, and the Franconia Inn, Horse & Hound, and Sugar Hill Inn have their own cross-country trails.

LOON MOUNTAIN

As much as Cannon Mountain is the embodiment of old New England skiing, Loon Mountain and Waterville Valley, the other major partners in the Ski 93 group, typify contemporary resort design. All three graze the 2,000-vertical-foot mark which delineates major eastern ski mountains from second-tier ones. While Cannon is solely a skiing mountain, the other two are full resorts. Loon and Waterville, which both opened in December 1966, installed snowmaking early and expanded it as necessary. Both include attractive developments of condominiums, mostly gray

*Loon Mountain's condominiums
and townhouses are first rate.*

clapboard or barn siding to blend with the New England setting, as well as health clubs, a choice of eating places, and night spots.

Like Cannon, Loon boasts two base areas, but there the resemblance ends. Loon's Octagon, a multi-purpose building at the base of the four-passenger gondola, is a short ride via a quaint shuttle train from the Governor Adams Lodge. In 1988, Loon replaced its twenty-one-year-old gondola with a new high-tech version. Medium-level skiing predominates, and only a handful of runs utilize the main mountain's entire 1,850-foot vertical.

Loon's remaining two hundred vertical feet are obtained by adding the top of North Peak, a small complex of tough terrain opened in 1984-85 to offer challenging bump skiing for experts. Tucked in a hollow at the bottom of the North Peak triple chair is another lodge, a log cabin called Camp 3 after an old logging camp. But with its yuppie menu that includes chili and chowder, quiche and wine, Camp 3's rusticity is only superficial. In March, when the steep top sections of Walking Boss and Flume are blessed with corn snow and the sun warms the earth, North Peak and the large sheltered terrace of Camp 3 define what spring skiing pleasure is all about.

Located along the Kancamagus Highway, a scenic east-west route through the White Mountains, Loon is the most central of the Ski 93 resorts.

LODGING

Condominiums and townhouses, from extremely comfortable to quite luxurious, prevail, both at Loon's base and a short ride away. The Mountain Club on Loon (formerly called the Inn at Loon Mountain), recently expanded and renovated, boasts a health club, indoor swimming pool, and sauna. Rachel's Dining Room serves American fare, and the Granite Bar is the resort's focal point for après-ski. In nearby Lincoln is The Homestead, a pleasant bed-and-breakfast inn, where skiers awaken to the aroma of fresh baking. The biggest motel in town is the Indian Head, halfway between Cannon and Loon, which has eighty-six units, an indoor pool complex, and a lounge with live entertainment. The Common Man is a popular country-style restaurant specializing in steaks and classic American fare. Après-skiers gather around a huge stone fireplace in the barn-size lounge.

WATERVILLE VALLEY

Waterville Valley, the most southerly of Ski 93's big three, has an ambiance similar to Loon's, but the layout is different. Waterville Village is strung through a broad valley. There, in the nineteenth century, a small inn was built but was destroyed by fire in 1886. It was replaced by a genteel hotel called the Waterville Inn, catering to summer guests interested in fishing, tennis, golf, and cool mountain air. By the mid-1930s, people were hiking up and skiing down old logging roads, and in 1938, the inn stayed open through the winter to house them. A year later, the Civilian Conservation Corps cut a real ski trail on Mount Tecumseh, a high peak across the valley, and a decade after that, a rope tow was run up Snow's Mountain behind the inn.

Twenty years later, Tom Corcoran, a two-time Olympian, Dartmouth grad, Harvard M.B.A., and buddy of assorted Boston Kennedys, purchased the Waterville Inn in order to develop a new type

*Mount Tecumseh in the
White Mountains is a
medium-size mountain that skis big.*

of ski resort. Sel Hannah was called upon to design the ski area, and new accommodations were built due to another fire, which destroyed the century-old Waterville Inn.

SKIING

When people speak of skiing Waterville, they mean Tecumseh, a medium-size mountain so cleverly configured that it skis big. It also has a world-wide reputation because, thanks to Corcoran's enterprise, it has hosted both Alpine and Nordic World Cup races.

Skiers park in lots terraced onto the hillside like tiers of a wedding cake. Open shuttles ferry them to the base lodge. From there it's up a series of lifts to an engaging mix of terrain. Novice slopes are conveniently and mercifully isolated from the intimidating traffic of faster skiers. There is a lot at Waterville for intermediates, plus a cluster of short headwalls that racers and good recreational skiers love. The High Country Express, a new high-speed quad, brings skiers to a slew of top-to-bottom routes, snowfields, meadows, cruising trails, and cut-offs. Two parallel Valley Run chairs do double duty to serve long, low-intermediate trails and also to feed into the Sunnyside triple, which in turn leads to Waterville's most difficult runs: Gema, True Grit, Ciao, and Bobby's Run.

Waterville's trails are engagingly named, often for people Corcoran wished to honor. Sel's Choice is for Sel Hannah, and Bobby's Run is for the late Robert F. Kennedy. Tyler Too and Terry's Trail are for a pair of New Hampshire twins, Terry and Tyler Palmer, stars of the U.S. Ski Team in the early seventies.

The Sunnyside and North Side chairlifts all unload on a small plateau where lucky skiers will find a seat in the Schwinde Hutte. This exquisite lunch spot is an adaptation of the Swiss-Romansch *Schwendis*, small restaurants scattered about the mountains to dispense hearty food and bracing refreshment. Waterville's version serves robust sausages, lovely quiche, and excellent lobster bisque. Above the hut is the short High Country chair, serving three neat intermediate trails and a steep glade. Snow's Mountain, its rope tow long ago replaced by a chair, is a weekend and holiday overflow area for beginners, who share the base facilities with cross-country skiers setting out on Waterville's 100-km trail network.

LODGING AND APRÈS-SKI

The Waterville resort, a mile and a half from the mountain, centers around a cluster of congenial lodges. The Snowy Owl, a modern yet countrified inn, is the finest of the group. The rooms surround an atrium-style lobby. Hyatt it's not, but convivial it is when a roaring fire and après-ski wine conspire to bring a glow to a skier's cheeks. Ultra-luxurious rooms in the new wing boast wet bars and private whirlpools. The Valley Inn and Tavern attracts the jocks with its indoor-outdoor heated pool, workout room, platform tennis, Jacuzzi, and sauna facilities—and full-service restaurant to sate the hunger all that activity works up. The Silver Squirrel is a small hospitable plant-filled aerie with a relaxed, quiet atmosphere. Other accommodations are condominium-style, including the spiffy new Golden Eagle Lodge, a condo-hotel with an indoor pool and pleasant lobby.

The Finish Line is an informal, pleasant family-style restaurant at Snow's Mountain, while O'Keefe's is a more ambitious eating place in the heart of the village. Both also have après-ski entertainment. Waterville offers Ski 93's greatest variety of non-ski activities, such as horsedrawn sleighs and skating on an indoor Olympic-size rink, and in 1986 it opened a new Sports Center, with racquet-sports courts and a complete health and fitness center.

BRETTON WOODS AND TENNEY MOUNTAIN

Bretton Woods, northeast of Franconia, is also in the Ski 93 family. The 1,500-vertical-foot mountain, offering skiing from very easy to moderately challenging, is surrounded by the White Mountain National Forest. One hundred kilometers of outstanding cross-country trails meander through the 2,600-acre property of the historic Mount Washington Inn, which hosted the Bretton Woods Conference that established the International Monetary Fund. The hotel, a white frame behemoth, is not winterized, which leaves skiers a choice of the fifty-room Lodge at Bretton Woods, the Rosebrook Townhouses, or the new Forest Cottages—low-key surroundings more conducive to quiet family outings than to high resort living. In the shadow of Mount Washington, the highest mountain east of the Mississippi, Bretton Woods benefits from the highest annual snowfall of any area in New Hampshire.

Down at the other end of the chain is Tenney Mountain, an on-again, off-again participant in the Ski 93 marketing effort. Similar in size, scale, and flavor to Bretton Woods, it changed hands in the mid-eighties and has embarked on an expansion program that has so far resulted in upgraded lifts, fifty more acres of terrain, and the construction of condominiums at the base.

Ski 93, built up for weekends, offers vacation variety. The quintessential New England experience, typified by Franconia and Cannon, appeals to fit and rugged folks seeking high-challenge skiing and low-key nightlife. Loon and Waterville are fine full-service resorts of a type that could be developed anywhere but happen to be near each other in north-central New Hampshire. Not surprisingly, they are the top two ski areas in the state in terms of annual skier visits. And Bretton Woods and Tenney are especially uncrowded during the week and appeal to parents and their offspring.

Ski The Summit, Colorado

A SHORT DRIVE FROM DENVER,
ANY ONE OF THE SKI THE SUMMIT
AREAS COULD MAKE IT ONTO A
LIST OF THE BEST SKI RESORTS
IN AMERICA

It is little longer than a commuting hop from Denver to Breckenridge, Copper Mountain, and Keystone—a trio of consummate recreational skiers' mountains. The three ski areas compete fiercely for the locals from Denver and environs on the east side of the Rockies. But for vacationers, they issue a joint multi-day lift pass and underwrite free bus service among the three areas and to the nearby towns of Dillon, Frisco, and Silverthorne.

Denver is served by direct flights from nearly everywhere. The three resorts are an easy drive through the Eisenhower Tunnel, an engineering marvel along Interstate 70, which bores under the Continental Divide, spilling vehicles into Summit County without having to negotiate a mountain pass. No wonder three million skier visits a year are tallied by the Ski the Summit resorts— nearly one-third of the total for all of Colorado—and more than the entire state of Utah. Proximity— plus aggressive promotion of steeply discounted lift tickets sold everywhere from ski shops to supermarkets—lure Front Range skiers. But the proximity to Stapleton Airport with no plane change

Maintained for use by skaters, Keystone Lake is America's largest ice rink.

appeals to outlanders as well.

No identical clones are these resorts. Breckenridge's dolled-up Main Street is a fine example of authentic Victorian gingerbread surrounded by a huge choice of modern hotels and condominiums. The other two resorts were built for skiing. Modern mid-rise condos and America's only Club Med ski village stretch along the base of Copper Mountain, one of the country's best-designed mountains. Keystone is a sparkling contemporary village built around a picturesque lake. An elegant hotel and attractive condominiums nestle in the woods. Six miles away, tucked against the Continental Divide, is Arapahoe Basin, a pristine Alp-like satellite owned by Keystone.

KEYSTONE

Keystone is the closest to Denver, requiring a short backtrack from the interstate up old U.S. Route 6. (On a clear day, one can skip the interstate altogether taking Route 6 over Loveland Pass, with its wild scenery, past A-Basin to Keystone.) The resort operates as if it were two hotels—one the highly honored Keystone Lodge and the other a network of secluded condominiums with a round-the-clock central front desk and switchboard. A fleet of buses connects the village center with Keystone's own area and Arapahoe Basin.

Keystone Mountain began to take shape in the late sixties when Max Dercum, one of the true visionaries of modern resort development, began laying out a ski area on a heavily wooded hump in sleepy Summit County. Dercum, a longtime ski school director, envisioned a mountain that met the needs of the masses of people taking up skiing in the sixties and early seventies. He felt they would want a wholly hospitable mountain—not one with a small novice section tucked into one corner of a challenging ski area, but a place totally comfortable for less-than-highly-skilled skiers.

Keystone Mountain, whose only steeps are confined to a wide trough on the eastern edge, proved ideal. Dercum's vision became reality with such runs as Schoolmarm, a three-mile trail down the whole 2,340-foot vertical; with Spring Dipper, Jay Bird, and Last Chance covering as much ground horizontally as they do vertically; and with Packsaddle Bowl, hollowed out of the ski area's left shoulder, served by its own double chairlift. Almost every skiable acre that isn't marked green carries a legitimate blue square. The intermediate trails range from the easy light blues of Hoo Doo and Grassy Thompson to the dark blues of Bachelor and Flying Dutchman which are not only steeper but also sometimes moguled. Keystone's meticulous grooming renders nearly everything but the half-dozen or so advanced runs within intermediate ability level.

Keystone installed the first sizable snowmaking system in Colorado, and was therefore better prepared for the lean snow seasons of 1975-76 and 1980-81 than its competitors. It now is regularly the first Colorado ski area to open (Halloween at Keystone is something of a tradition).

While the Ralston Purina Company bought Keystone in 1983, the only indication of their ownership is that the beginner slope is called Checkerboard Flats; but greater financial backing has ensured steady growth and consistent commitment to quality. Keystone has refined the concept of the user-friendly ski area, adding such niceties as billboard-size letters on trail signs, thick pads on chairlift seats, and free Kleenex in the lift mazes.

In 1978, Keystone bought Arapahoe Basin, America's highest lift-served ski area. The base elevation of this pristine powder pocket is at a (literally) breathtaking 10,780 feet above sea level—and its lifts top out at 12,450. A-Basin is the run Pallavicini, 1,300 vertical feet of steady, massively moguled fall-line skiing. It is The Alleys, a quartet of perilous glades that cling to the edge of the Basin. And it is the East Wall, a sublime steep face for powder skiing. Arapahoe also has some easier terrain, and even intermediates who have acclimated to the altitude ought to spend at least part of a sunny day revelling in the sense of apartness and drinking in the exhilarating views.

In 1984, Keystone spent $15 million for new lifts, including two triple chairlifts, and the purchase of 1,620 vertical foot North Peak, an adjacent summit with steep terrain. Where Keystone Mountain is super-groomed, North Peak's seven trails sprout enough moguls to bring a gleeful gleam to bumpers' eyes. Experts begin the day with a waltz from the summit of Keystone Mountain down Mozart or Diamond Back to catch the morning's best powder. They ride the Santiago triple all day and yoyo North Peak's steeps, using the Teller chair to the Keystone summit only for a pit stop, lunch, or the end-of-the-day run down the main mountain.

APRÈS-SKI AND OTHER ACTIVITIES

For some people, the best after ski activity is more skiing. For them, Keystone has Colorado's largest night-skiing installation with the gondola and a half-dozen runs open nightly. The touring center, under the direction of Jana Hlavaty, an ebullient Czech-born racer (she was naturalized just in time to be on the 1976 U.S. Olympic Team), runs outstanding excursions including ski trips to old mining towns and moonlight tours into the Arapaho National Forest.

Keystone has tennis on two indoor courts, horsedrawn sleighrides to a hearty dinner in an old ranch house, swimming in eleven heated pools, and skating on the country's largest maintained ice rink, the frozen surface of Keystone Lake. These activities help make Keystone a resort that appeals to all ages—one with a noteworthy children's program and a thriving teen center.

LODGING AND RESTAURANTS

The lakeside Keystone Lodge, honored with five diamonds from AAA and four stars from *Mobil Travel Guide,* is contemporary yet offers old-fashioned service. The Lodge's Garden Room, a spacious, glassed-in aerie serves fine continental-style food. Nearby, Ski Tip Lodge, an 1860s stagecoach stop restored by Max and Edna Dercum into a casual ski lodge, also serves excellent food in a low-key setting. Keystone Ranch, by contrast, is classy, an exquisitely crafted adaptation of rusticity that presents first-rate cuisine, an excellent wine list, and top service during its two nightly seatings.

BRECKENRIDGE

Breckenridge was named after John C. Breckinridge, James Buchanan's vice president (and later re-spelled). The town was hit with gold fever in 1859. And on July 23, 1887, Tom Graves, working in the Gold Flake Mine, unearthed the largest gold nugget ever found in Colorado—weighing thirteen pounds, seven ounces troy. In 1898, an Englishman named Ben Stanley Revett brought a fleet of nine mining dredges to cull ore from the beds of the Swan and Blue rivers and in French Gulch. The dredges inched their way through the valley for decades. When it became known that the richest ore lay under Main Street, plans were made to demolish the old houses and begin digging. The town was spared only because the last dredge was melted down in 1943 for the war effort.

Where Keystone plays its melodies in soft harmony, nearby Breckenridge offers a jazzy dissonance. The approach on Route 9 is flanked by mounds of snow-covered mine tailings, a remnant of the area's past. Main Street, a vibrant avenue lined with attractively restored nineteenth-century buildings, invites strolling and shopping and just hanging out. The surrounding condos are convenient and functional.

The ski town was not always this way, however. The establishment of the area coincided with the counterculture sixties and turned downtown Breckenridge—which had once been almost a ghost town—into a hippie haven. Those wild days are now history, and landmark legislation dictates how each building may be decorated. Pressing in on the original old town is by far the biggest resort in Summit County, with accommodations for 23,000 visitors. The natural wood, neutral gray, and occasional natural stone favored by architects of high-rise Breckenridge inch up against Peak 8, Peak 9, and Peak 10, the southernmost summits of the Ten Mile Range, which comprise the ski area.

SKIING

Three chairlifts on Peak 8, the first developed, access a splay of novice-to-intermediate runs. Even the more difficult are steep only on top with long, flat runouts. Breckenridge's best skiers regard Peak 8 only as a conduit to a summit T-bar which rides a ridge and serves super-steep bowls on either side. The front face consists of Contest Bowl and Horseshoe Bowl, two treeless craters that earn their double-black diamonds. Peak 9's North Face has hairy chutes and glades. To ski Mine Shaft, Devil's Crotch, Satan's Inferno, and Tom's Baby is to be in the company of Breckenridge's hotshots. To ski them well is to earn their respect. This extreme skiing, topping out at 12,213 feet, is exhilarating for those who can manage it, but in mid-winter, when the powder might be the best, the wind-plagued upper lifts are often closed.

A handful of ultra-steep bump runs spill off the top of Peak 8 into the valley that separates it from the Peak 9 summit. A monster mogul run called Mach 1 is one venue of the annual World Cup Freestyle bump competition. (The aerial and ballet segments are held on the milder terrain of Peak 9.) It is Peak 9 that has given Breckenridge its reputation as an easy ski area with acres of tame terrain that is excellent for beginners and perennial intermediates, who can feel like king of the hill on the entire carefully groomed 1,860-foot vertical.

What Breckenridge long needed was something more challenging than Peak 9 and both less weather-vulnerable and less difficult than the Peak 8 bowls—single black diamonds below the timberline rather than doubles above it. This need was well filled with expansion in 1985-86 to Peak 10, a ridge with steep fall-aways on both sides. Peak 10's spindly chutes breed tight moguls, and there are terrific tree runs and a wide powder slope called The Burn that catches the new snow blowing off the ridge top and offers nirvana among the well-spaced trees.

But it was lift development rather than trail cutting that ensured Breckenridge's place in ski history, specifically the installation in 1984-85 of the continent's first high-speed detachable quad chair on Peak 9. The following winter, Vail installed four high-speeders on more difficult terrain and turned the ski world on its ear by dramatically paring lines and offering skiers more runs per day. Breckenridge countered by converting the Peak 10 quad to detachable and building a new super chair on Peak 8.

OTHER ACTIVITIES

In 1936, a local women's club, contending that Breckenridge had never officially become part of Colorado, had asked the state to allow it to act as a "free and independent Kingdom" for three days each year. Those three days were devoted to the Ullr Dag Festival, named for the Nordic god who protects skiers—and that tradition continues to the present. The week-long Ullr Fest each January features ice sculptures, parades, fireworks, a torchlight parade, and other winter merriment. Actually, merriment reigns in Breckenridge all season long. In addition to such pleasures as swimming, sauna-ing, hot tubbing, and working out, there is skating on Maggie Pond and cross-country, Sno-Coach tours and snowmobiling at Tiger Run, the country's largest snowmobile center. Breckenridge is also a town for great shopping, from tacky T-shirts to trendy fashions and original art.

LODGING AND RESTAURANTS

There is elegant dining (Spencer's, the Polo Club, the St. Bernard Inn, and the Briar Rose), but most of the eating places are more casual. Fatty's broils big burgers and bakes a variety of pizzas. And Horseshoe II has a large selection of inexpensive sandwiches and entrées. The party crowd does its after-skiing to live rock bands at the Mogul at Georgian Square, the Village Pub, and Shamus O'Toole's.

Breckenridge also offers Summit County's greatest array of lodging. Nowhere else can skiers choose between the Brown Hotel and Beaver Run—and everything in between. When it was built in 1890, Brown's boasted that it had the only bathtub in Summit County. Today it is a lovely inn and restaurant. Beaver Run, however, is what Franz Kafka would have come up with had he imagined an American ski hotel. This slopeside behemoth boasts more than five hundred condo units, six outdoor hot tubs, city-size exercise facilities, one of the largest convention centers in the Rockies, and the world's largest indoor mini-golf course.

COPPER MOUNTAIN

Copper Mountain, near the eastern end of Vail Pass, traces its history back even further than Breckenridge. During excavation for the foundation of a ski-area base building, workers unearthed the remains of a prehistoric bison and some stone tools presumably used by early Indian settlers. The site is known to have been continuously settled from about 7320 B.C. to 1740 A.D. Later, Ute Indians, French trappers, copper miners, railroad pioneers, and ranchers took their turns— James Michener's *Centennial* comes to life at this place, which was known to early Coloradans as Wheeler Junction.

In 1969, the United States Forest Service, which is empowered to grant special-use permits for public land, declared: "If ever there was a mountain that had terrain for skiing, it would be Copper Mountain. It is probably the most outstanding potential ski area available in the Arapaho National Forest and possibly Colorado. The area will lie adjacent to Interstate 70 at Wheeler Junction."

SKIING

Modern history began on December 5, 1972, when 135 people skied on opening day of Copper Mountain, seventy-five miles from Denver. Copper, the most compact of the Ski the Summit trio, is a small, planned village ranging along the base of an excellent all-around ski mountain. The trails, neat as tenpins, fan out logically, as a card player arranges a hand. Facing the mountain, the most difficult trails are clustered on the left, the intermediate runs are in the middle, and the novice turf is on the right. Only about one third of the terrain, however, is visible from the base. Union Peak and Spaulding Bowl loom pristine and white above and behind the main face. On this mountain, skiers know at the beginning of a run that they are going to end up on the same kind of terrain they started on. Where there is a mid-trail option, the choice is between two with the same difficulty. Copper offers a lot of interest but few surprises.

The beginner terrain is exemplary, the intermediate trails are long and sweet, and the expert terrain is underrated. Where other major mountains have a signature run whose name comes easily to mind—like Exhibition at Sun Valley or Riva Ridge at Vail, like Ruthie's at Aspen or Al's at Taos—Copper doesn't have a truly famous one. The closest is Rosi's Run, a bottom-of-the-mountain pitch named after the great West German racer Rosi Mittermaier, winner of two Olympic golds and a silver. But Rosi's is just one of four medium and four long black runs that slash dramatically through the thick woods to the base area.

More difficult and more dramatic terrain is found way up top. The upper sections of the highest peak are open powder bowls, while the lower parts are in the trees. Spaulding Bowl is scooped out below the rim of Copper Mountain, the peak that gave its name to the resort. The timberline hits fast, as the broad bowl suddenly funnels into Widowmaker, a narrow run that then snakes around islands of fir trees. On the same mountain face is Resolution Bowl, which tapers into a choice of three demanding trails.

In just nine minutes, Copper's American Flyer high-speed quad carries skiers from the base of the mountain into Union Bowl, a steep hollow below the summit of Union Peak. On this face, the trees begin to fill in the bowl's lower section, providing classy glade skiing. While most of Union is unquestionably difficult, Wheeler Creek and Union Park are high gentle glades on the bowl's edge that offer the high-mountain experience to intermediates.

Nine out of ten ski resorts claim to be dedicated to family skiing, but Copper really is. Untold numbers of skiing parents have parked their infants in Belly Button Babies or their toddlers in the Belly Button Bakery while they went off to ski. Copper was one of the first resorts to start three-year-olds on skis—and still is one of the rare ones to have special classes for youngsters from pre-schoolers all the way up through hot-skiing teenagers.

LODGING AND RESTAURANTS

Also convenient for families is Copper's compact, walk-about layout. The condos and condo-hotels are largely interchangeable, with location and amenities more than style determining which one is preferred. The exception is the 225-room, self-contained Franco-American Club Med, run on the all-inclusive theme that Club Med has successfully transplanted from the tropics to the slopeside. And a new Hyatt, the first in ski country, is slated for the heart of the village.

In naming places, Copper's management has a penchant for using the definite article. The base lodge, called The Center, is used not only for skiing but for a variety of après-ski entertainment. The top-of-the-line continental restaurant is called The Plaza. Three informal meals a day, with a Mexican accent, are served in The Clubhouse. Ice cream and light lunches are offered at The Scoop.

OTHER ACTIVITIES

Copper attracts jocks drawn not only by the mountain but also by the best fitness center in Summit County. It features two indoor tennis courts, two racquetball courts, a lushly landscaped year-round pool, mirrored workout studio, Nautilus and free-weight rooms, hot tubs, sauna, steamroom, tanning beds, and massage. Also popular is Rackets', the spa's full-service restaurant and sports bar. Carousing is relatively mild, for Copper Mountain types would rather do arm curls with a five-pound dumbbell than with a beer mug.

Any one of the Ski the Summit villages could make it into a list of the best ski resorts of North America. To get them all on one interchangeable lift ticket so close to Denver is no less than a knockout.

Snowbird & Alta, Utah

WITH AN AVERAGE SNOWFALL
OF FIVE HUNDRED INCHES A YEAR,
THEY ARE RECOGNIZED AS AMERICA'S
UNRIVALED POWDER CAPITALS

In the skiing world, the Rockies are famous for the quantity and quality of their powder snow. Within the Rockies, Utah's Wasatch Range is famous for its powder. And within the Wasatch, Little Cottonwood Canyon, just southeast of Salt Lake City, is famous for its powder. At the head of Little Cottonwood, just a mile apart, are Snowbird and Alta, which average five hundred inches of snowfall per year. Not surprisingly they are recognized as America's unrivaled powder capitals.

Each of these tiny resorts huddles at the base of an extraordinary ski mountain. Their histories, their operations, their characters are as different as yin and yang, yet they complement each other like peanut butter and jelly. (These two, plus Solitude and Brighton in Big Cottonwood Canyon and Park City, ParkWest, and Deer Valley in Parley's Canyon, are skiable on an interchangeable lift pass.)

Alta is one of America's oldest ski areas. Neither the mountain nor the lodging has changed much in decades. The resort is a study in anti-chic. Each of the four lodges is privately managed, distinctive in style, and unique in its policies. The ski area's lift-ticket pricing is simple: full-day

Bring your snorkel
for the possible four-foot dump.

and half-day tickets for adults and children—no midweek and weekend differential, no early- or late-season breaks, no multi-day discounts, just bargain rates. Alta doesn't even take credit cards.

Snowbird is younger. Its four high-rise, architecturally harmonious lodges are managed by the mountain company. The complicated price structure that prevails in other American resorts does so at Snowbird: half-day, one-day, and multi-day; adults, kids, and senior citizens; chairlifts only or tram included; early season and late season. And plastic is welcome.

SNOWBIRD

It's official name is Snowbird Ski & Summer Resort, but no one calls it that. Knowing skiers refer to this bit of heaven in the Wasatch as "The Bird"—as in "The Big, Beautiful Bird." And there's nothing like The Bird's 3,100 vertical feet of magic, an ethereal world blanketed in downy white, somewhere between the earth and sky. Jonathan Livingston Skier, this is it.

The Bird's demanding terrain is accessed by the Snowbird tram.

SKIING

The base hub is Snowbird Center, a mini-mall of shops and restaurants, from which a 125-passenger aerial tram climbs to the sky-high peaks and heavenly skiing. The tram sails swiftly over a spiny ridge, anchoring the 11,000-foot summit of Hidden Peak to the valley below. Half-way through the eight-minute ride, the ridge arcs into a wide reverse-C, enfolding a great bowl. The walls of the bowl, which the map calls the Cirque, appear too steep to ski; but passengers can spot an occasional small figure trailing rooster tails of powder from the hard check which must complete each turn.

Sometimes the tram ride may have the boisterous ambiance of a fraternity beer blast; other times, especially when the car is filled with a new crop of vacationers, or during a storm when snowflakes the size of nickels swirl outside the windows, the car is as hushed as a chapel. Some skiers appear awed at being at one of skiing's holy places. Others are fervently asking themselves, "Oh God, what am I doing here?"

The tram unloads on a small plateau atop Hidden Peak. Spread below is some of the best, most demanding skiing in the world. There are three ways down: skiing the Peruvian or the Gad sides of the ridge, which is like choosing between ecstasy and rapture; or swallowing one's pride and riding the tram down again.

By Snowbird standards, Peruvian's main run and a couple of detours off it are rated "more difficult," but they would be unabashed expert terrain on most other mountains of the world. The upper section is a stadium-shaped bowl as awesome from the ground as it appears from the tram above. Chip's Run starts as a cat-track into the deepest part of the bowl and continues down the path of least steepness. Ultra-experts may take a high line to ski Upper Cirque, Great Scott, or Silver Fox, absolutely dizzying drops off the rim. Others take Chip's as it snakes to the canyon floor, providing them with glimpses of the black-diamond runs. After all, it is one thing to admire the tracks, chutes, and headwalls that don't even show on the trail map; it is another thing for most mortals to consider skiing them.

Three-quarters of the way down, Peruvian, which starts as such a wide bowl on top, pleats into a series of steep, narrow rills to the base. The Peruvian chairlift accesses this lower section, offering tough chute and mogul skiing. Lower Peruvian is especially popular on days when visibility on top is zero—or when the tram is weathered in altogether.

While Peruvian makes a pretense of offering some quasi-intermediate skiing, the upper Gad doesn't sport a single blue square. The main attraction is Regulator Johnson, a quarter-mile-wide treeless slope. Some days it is Utah's broadest mogul field. At other times, under a mantle of new snow, it is a peerless powder slope. In spring when the snow has corned up, Regulator Johnson is a cruising hill smooth as Breyer's vanilla. On the far side is Little Cloud, another steep, sensational snowfield served by a double chair which operates until June, for one of America's longest ski seasons.

The Gad side is not only larger than Peruvian, it provides more variety too. It is served by five double chairlifts. The Wilbere is the lowest, accessing just a handful of runs, but it is located practically in the center of the base area and acts as a relay between the tram base and two other chairs, Mid-Gad and Gad I. These lifts, which parallel one another, serve the lower portion of Gad Valley, which includes Big Emma, a smooth boulevard marked with a green circle, which

Après-ski at Aspen's Little Nell's.

The town of Aspen as seen from Ruthie's Run.

The Village Mall at Snowmass.

The tram as seen from East Ridge Traverse.

An elkhorn arch, an artifact of the once wild West, is located in the town of Jackson.

Teton Village at sunset.

Sunrise Village is one of the few condominum developments that is adjacent to the ski area.

A skier descends Goat Path.

Taking a break from the bumps on Bear Mountain.

Members of the U.S. Ski Team at Alpine Meadows.

Many skiers enjoy the nightlife at the casinos on the South Shore.

Alpine's facilities include sun decks and barbecue stations.

Heavenly Valley's slopes offer breathtaking views of Lake Tahoe and South Shore hotels and casinos.

Deer Valley in Utah's Wasatch Range.

Park City's Main Street.

The four-passenger gondola is one of Park City's oldest lifts.

An old mining building is part of Park City's history.

The runs serviced by the four-passenger gondola at Loon Mountain are popular with intermediate skiers.

Cannon Mountain presents some of New England's most demanding terrain.

The Waterville Valley base lodge, a familiar place to some of Boston's Brahmins.

Copper Mountain, which was well planned, has become an excellent all-around ski area.

Breckenridge is a historic western town that is now surrounded by a large ski resort with a wide variety of accommodations.

Ski touring at Keystone includes trips to old mining towns and tours by moonlight.

Snowbird lodges are high-rise rather than quaint, but they offer excellent amenities.

Powder hounds in heaven.

"The Bird" nestled in Little Cottonwood Canyon.

At Steamboat guests can ski with Billy Kidd, one of the legends of American skiing.

Great skiing and a friendly atmosphere bring vacationers back again and again.

Since 1980 nearly $30 million has been spent to improve the mountain and its facilities.

STOWE, VERMONT

The classic New England village of Stowe.

Because of its mountain, its facilities, and its history, Stowe is often referred to as the ski capital of the East.

The Trapp Family Lodge, founded by the same family whose talent was enshrined in The Sound of Music, combines the best styles of New England and Austria.

The mountain says, "Ski me if you can."

Many of the regular skiers at Sugarloaf have rugged constitutions and sharp edges.

Training the next generation.

The village is a warm oasis for chilled skiers.

would be a blue square on most mountains. Gad II, a mid-mountain lift, veers off to some sensational glade skiing. The only true beginner terrain is Chickadee, a small practice slope beside the Cliff Lodge, suitable for children's and first-timers' classes.

The most subtly named run is S.T.H. That stands for Straight To Hell, so be forewarned. The most engagingly named is Bassackwards, after Dick Bass, the Texas millionaire who built Snowbird in 1972. Bass is a legend, having climbed Mt. Everest at age fifty-five, becoming the oldest man to do so and coincidentally becoming the first to ascend the highest peaks on each of the seven continents.

Snowbird was a pioneer in initiating free daily meet-the-mountain tours. A fresh-faced host or hostess introduces this complex mountain, pointing out the easiest routes in each section, explaining what has and what hasn't been groomed, and answering questions about the resort. But the essence of The Bird can't be found in the company of a group shepherded along the thirty-nine marked trails. The real Snowbird is the ungroomed acreage, a compelling smorgasbord of secret chutes, dense glades, and startling headwalls. This terrain lures even very good skiers back to ski school—to find an instructor not only able to help with powder and backcountry technique but also willing to duck under the snow-clad lower branches of a stand of barrier firs to lead an advanced class into the untracked world beyond the trees.

The longtime ski school director, Junior Bounous, is one of the world's great powder skiers, and the instructors he hires are ultimate powderhounds, too. Business is good at the Snowbird Ski School.

LODGING

Business is also good at the Cliff Lodge, the largest and poshest of the four accommodations. The Cliff took on a stunning new dimension in 1987 with a $67-million, thirteen-story addition, comprised of luxurious guest rooms (for a total of 532), an eleven-story atrium, and a bi-level, health-and-beauty spa. It is possible to work out in a weight room or aerobics studio with the inspirational panorama of the Wasatch visible through floor-to-ceiling picture windows. Or swim in a fifty-four-foot rooftop lap pool—or soak with two dozen other sybarites in a huge outdoor whirlpool. Massage, hydro-massage, herbal wraps, or an exotic European treatment called parafango (a relaxing application of hot wax and volcanic ash) do wonders to unkink a tight body. The beauty salon offers a complete range of hair, nail, and skin care to make spa clients look as good as they feel. Within a few weeks of the spa's inauguration, the health and beauty programs were heavily booked—both by fitness-minded skiers and by non-skiers who prefer the mountains to the desert.

From the outside, the three other lodges look much like smaller versions of the Cliff—solid, functional blocks of concrete designed to blend in with the granite outcroppings. The Lodge at Snowbird, the Inn, and the Iron Blosam are condominium buildings with deluxe rooms and suites.

Wherever visitors lay their heads, chances are they will wake up to the muffled sounds of howitzers and grenades set off by the Ski Patrol to blast the night's accumulation of snow off avalanche-prone sections of the mountains before the lifts open. Morning activity starts early at Snowbird, not just with the patrol, but also with the line that forms for the first tram ride. These are skiers anxious for first tracks in what, day after day, is a velvety blanket of fresh powder. Even those who don't feel compelled to be on the first tram ride get going early, for Snowbird attracts skiers first and partyers hardly at all. Après-ski, therefore, peaks early. The noisiest night spot, especially for the young group, is the Tram Room, which rocks loudly. The Lodge Club in the Lodge at Snowbird and the Eagle's Nest Lounge at the Cliff draw a more sedate, older crowd.

RESTAURANTS

Snowbird's signature restaurant is The Aerie, a new multi-level restaurant atop the Cliff Lodge, done in trendy tones of forest green and plum, and serving New American Cuisine. The sprightly Spa Cafe serves calorie-controlled meals, big on fish, vegetable dishes, pasta, and stuff with sprouts. The Wildflower, an informal Italian restaurant in the Iron Blosam, has earned fast favor with families. The Steak Pit in Snowbird Center and the highly lauded Mexican Keyhole, also at the Cliff Lodge, are self-explanatory. Light dinners are available at the Forklift in Snowbird Center and The Atrium in the Cliff.

Many experts are addicted to Alta.

ALTA

It is possible, though generally not advisable, to ski from Snowbird to Alta. Most people drive up-canyon—a wise move. The destination is a huddle of lodges which look as if they were flung randomly by some giant at the foot of the rock cliffs. Looming above these buildings is the snowy wall of Alf's High Rustler, one of the steepest and most intimidating ski slopes in America.

Alta is the ultimate traditional resort. There are no high-tech lifts, no central base lodge, and no master-plan. There are four lodges, a couple of other small structures, and lots of parking lots. To get into an inn may require climbing down a long flight of stairs, roofed over for avalanche protection. To get from the inn to the base of the lifts means more downhill. And to move along the base area means grabbing hold of one of the horizontal rope tows that take two-way traffic. As a resort, Alta is best characterized by what it doesn't have; it doesn't have sushi bars, pick-up bars, high-rise condos, high-fashion ski outfits, video parlors, tennis courts, skating rinks, horsedrawn sleigh rides, art galleries, or boutiques. But Alta does have some of the best skiing in the world.

In 1938, old mining machinery was used to piece together the Collins single chairlift—America's third chair—to ferry skiers up a mountain overlooking an old mining camp. The tariff was fifteen cents a ride. The Collins lift, now a double, is still there, along with seven other double chairs on a 2,000-foot vertical.

SKIING

Day skiers may start on the Albion side, but vacationers tend to roll out of the lodges and straight to the Wildcat or Collins chair. From there, they hit the Germania lift, serving a bowl snugged into a hollow below the summit of Mt. Baldy and some awe-inspiring ungroomed terrain. Mambo and Ballroom are aptly named sections of the bowl, for they invite skiers to kick up their heels a bit. Alta aficionados hit the High Traverse, which leads to Alf's High Rustler, Eagles' Nest, Greeley Bowl, North Rustler, and Stonecrusher, which—on a scale of one to ten—collectively rate a twenty. Sunspot, by no means an easy run, is the lightest of the lot. Hardcore ultra-experts with high quotients of stamina hike another hundred vertical feet or so to Eddie's High Nowhere for gut-busting, sublimely difficult skiing rarely found on this side of the Atlantic. Anyone considering tackling this terrain should remember that the only way out is to ski. If in doubt about the snow conditions, check with the patrol—and then believe whatever they tell you.

Much of the Albion side is considerably milder—even legitimately intermediate. Albion Basin, a teacup-shaped upper bowl of astonishing scenic splendor, features Roller Coaster and Devil's Elbow off the Supreme lift; and Rock 'n Roll and Big Dipper off the Sugarloaf chair. They provide grand cruising, considerably more varied than most blue squares. Novice boulevards off the Albion and Sunnyside chairs are for those few new skiers who come to Alta, generally accompanying experts who would ski nowhere else.

LODGING

There is also a small army of regulars who would stay nowhere else. The four old-time ski lodges offer a surprising range of living styles from dorm to deluxe, all on full or modified American plan. The lodges' on-premises après-ski activities are so subdued that they make Snowbird seem positively wild.

The Alta Lodge, one of the world's great ski lodges, is the first among near-equals. Offering accommodations from deluxe rooms with fireplaces and balconies to spare bathless singles, this is a place that epitomizes the Alta style. The cuisine is commendable, the après-ski is heavy on conversation and light on noise and alcohol consumption, and the very air has a congenial bouquet. The ambiance recalls the old days of skiing, when inns were run by skiers who treated their clients like much-loved houseguests.

The Rustler Lodge is larger and, while also offering a range of accommodations, tends to be more luxurious. The closest thing to a trendy touch at Alta is the Rustler's three-story glassed-in addition, which provides diners with a matchless view of the mountain and of the lodge's large outdoor heated pool. The Alta Peruvian has an even bigger pool, plus a somewhat livelier atmosphere that draws a younger crowd. The Goldminer's Daughter, recently remodeled, is the simplest of the bunch. It also has a cafeteria and ski shop.

Blackjack, the Hellgate, and Powder Ridge are condominiums halfway between Alta and Snowbird. They have the space and economy condo dwellers prefer, but anywhere in Little Cottonwood Canyon, heavy snows sometimes mandate that everyone stay indoors until the patrol has finished blasting. And being snowed in at a convivial lodge is preferable to being trapped in a condo.

Without Alta, there might never have been a Snowbird. They are an ironic duo—so close physically yet so different philosophically—the odd couple of the snows. Sharing Little Cottonwood, they are cautious neighbors with little in common except proximity. Still, the people who run these two exceptional resorts, and the people who ski them, have great respect for one another. And the rest of the ski world stands in awe of them both.

Steamboat, Colorado

STEAMBOAT IS NOT ONLY
BIG-TIME BUT BIG-HEARTED
AS WELL. THE PLACE
RADIATES FRIENDLINESS

Even before you arrive at Steamboat, you will be aware it is determinedly western in flavor. Road signs urge you to visit F. M. Light & Son in Steamboat Springs for western wear, cowboy hats, and riding regalia. If you approach from the west—from the Yampa Valley Regional Airport at Hayden—you reach the town of Steamboat Springs first, its folksy main drag just the way you expected the home of F. M. Light to look. If you arrive from Denver or other points east, however, you first come upon the resort of Steamboat, a development stacked against the ski mountain, a sudden contrast to the ranch land and wilderness you've passed en route. Then, Light's signs seem as much a bit of charming artifice as cowboy hats on ski instructors.

In Steamboat Springs, located in northern Colorado where the mountains taper off into the high plains, Light's is for real, and ten-gallon hats do serve as working wear for authentic cowpokes and authentic ski instructors. When Billy Kidd, a native of Stowe, Vermont, and a 1964 Olympic silver medalist, became Steamboat's director of skiing, he made the cowboy hat his own trademark—and a symbol of the ski area as well.

The old barn is a picturesque Steamboat landmark.

Together, the town and resort accommodate nearly fifteen thousand guests. The ski area, one of Colorado's largest, is third after Vail and Snowmass in skiable acreage (1,551), tied with Copper Mountain for the most lifts (20), second behind Vail in uphill capacity (28,730 skiers per hour), and second behind Aspen Highlands in vertical drop (3,600 feet). Spread those impressive statistics over a four-peaked *massif*, build a bustling resort at the base, and link it with a real aw-shucks western town, and you have a winning combination.

Steamboat, remote from other resorts in the state, is so far up in north-central Colorado that it's almost in Wyoming. In this case, remoteness is not inaccessibility, and Steamboat has always been reasonably easy for vacationers to reach. Remoteness, however, does necessitate marketing acumen. So Steamboat was the first in Colorado to subsidize a major airline to schedule frequent jet service direct from its major markets. It also pioneered the Kids Ski Free concept, enabling a family of four to sleep, ski, and rent equipment for the price of just the two adults. Steamboat enjoys high repeat business and a splendid word-of-mouth reputation because it is not only big-time but big-hearted as well, radiating friendliness while it gives skiers a good time for their money.

Steamboat's famous
"champagne powder."

HISTORY

There was skiing at Steamboat Springs long before there was a ski area. Carl Howelson, a top Norwegian ski jumper, came to the United States in 1905 to perform "Ski Sailing, The Perilous Scandinavian Winter Sport in All Its Wild and Wondrous Daring" for the Barnum & Bailey Circus. During his travels, "the flying Norseman" helped organize ski clubs and develop ski-jumping facilities—in Steamboat Springs, among other places. In 1913, Howelson started a simple fun-filled winter carnival there for the locals. An updated version of this carnival is still on Steamboat Springs' calendar each February. Behind Main Street is a winter-recreation area—440 vertical feet of skiing, five ski jumps, ice skating, and a modest cross-country loop—named Howelson Hill. "Ski Town USA," as it sometimes calls itself, claims to have produced more Olympic skiers than any other ski area—sixteen at last count—and Howelson Hill is where they first learned to ski downhill and to jump.

In the early sixties, a group of local businessmen decided that the town ought to have more

Everyone gets into the western spirit.

skiing than Howelson Hill could offer. They built an A-frame at the base of Storm Mountain and put in a couple of surface lifts. Later the first chairlift was constructed, climbing from the current gondola base to open the "main mountain." In 1969, the LTV Corporation purchased the ski area and began what was to become a steady pattern of terrain expansion and lift additions with a new lift on the face of Storm Peak. LTV also developed a full resort village, which they named Steamboat. They subsequently strung new lifts on the Headwall and at Burgess Creek, and in 1970, Colorado's second gondola was installed (Vail's was the first).

The terrain on the Storm Peak summit, Priest Creek, and Sunshine Peak was added in the seventies, as were accommodations, shops, and restaurants at the base. Along with other ski resorts, Steamboat suffered from overbuilding and speculation in the early to mid-eighties. But much of this development has benefited skiers. Since 1980, nearly $30 million has been invested in snowmaking, expanded mountain restaurants, improved trail signs, vastly improved base facilities, a dozen new runs, five new chairlifts, upgrades of five existing chairlifts, and, of course, the Silver Bullet, the first eight-passenger gondola in North America.

The ski area now sprawls over four peaks—Thunderhead, Storm, Sunshine, and South. Thunderhead, the main mountain face, is easy to remember, because the Thunderhead Lodge, four stories of eating and drinking, is located where the gondola unloads. Storm and Sunshine each offer about 2,000 vertical feet of sublime skiing, while South Peak is a knoblet between the bottom of Sunshine and the top of Thunderhead.

SKIING

This multi-peak layout means that you never get a visual sense of how much terrain there really is. There is so much variety that neither its topography nor its skiable acreage nor even its lift system can be described in a neat phrase. Some lifts which load just a few hundred feet from one another diverge to serve totally different groups of trails. Others begin on opposite sides of a peak and meet at the top. And two pairs of chairs, Christie II and Christie III on lower Thunderhead and Sundown and Priest Creek on Sunshine, parallel each other and serve the same terrain.

Whether the trail map indicates that a run is "easier," "more difficult," or "most difficult," intermediate skiing predominates. At the low end of intermediate runs are BC Ski Way and Why Not, green-circle roads down Thunderhead, which are long and fun. At the higher end are Heavenly Daze or Valley View, which are steepish but wide and frequently groomed. In between are the blue-square runs off the far side of Sunshine chair, wide, gentle trails with non-stop views.

Powder aficionados revere Steamboat for its tree skiing—perhaps the greatest concentration of fine glades in Colorado. With the construction of the Priest Creek chair, the best glades are now the core of the upper mountain, drawing skiers who like to slalom through the firs and the aspens. Out of the trees, Twister, Hurricane, Tornado, and Cyclone get the bumps, while Chute One, The Ridge, and Crow Track are steep powder runs.

What unites the whole diversity of terrain at Steamboat is the effervescent snow—an average of 325 inches of it a year—usually so light that it has been nicknamed "champagne powder." Billy Kidd says it was the powder which lured him from Stowe, where status depended on ability to ski icy, mogully trails with control and speed. In his forties, with an emerging bald pate and three small children he dotes on, Billy today is a strong, graceful powder skier.

He is also the resort's most effective ambassador. Every day when he isn't away on some promotional tour, celebrity race, or other event, America's first male Olympic ski medalist arrives at the top of Thunderhead at 1:00 p.m. to ski with visitors. This gentle man leads them down a long gentle run like Why Not, talking about skiing generally or Steamboat specifically, giving a pointer to this skier, a word of encouragement to that one, or just a friendly word to another.

While Carl Howelson brought skiing and jumping to Steamboat Springs, Sven Wiik promoted another Nordic sport, cross-country skiing, in the rest of the Yampa Valley. His Scandinavian Lodge, tucked into the woods just west of the downhill runs, is a rustic charmer with fine trails outside the door. There is also an easy touring center on the golf course, and memorable, high-mountain excursions on Rabbit Ears Pass.

APRÈS-SKI

Steamboat Resort is a lively center for dining, bar-hopping, and simply strolling. Two handsome plazas, Ski Time Square and Gondola Square, are at the base of the mountain. The Tugboat Saloon is the traditional starting point for après-ski. It's a little rowdy and a lot of fun. The Sheraton has Buddy's Run, where happy hour features big-screen TV video highlights of the skiing day. Later, action at the Sheraton shifts to H.B. Longbaugh (Butch Cassidy's real name), where drinks, a munchie menu, and a casual ambiance are the lures. Hershies in the Clock Tower Building also has a big-screen TV, plus a super sound system for dancing into the night.

In town, the Steamboat Yacht Club, which says it accepts "only members and non-members," has terrific bar food, and live entertainment, while the Old Town Pub serves nightly drink specials in one of the oldest downtown buildings.

There is even a special, supervised after-ski place for youngsters. The SKIDS Club in Gondola Square dispenses snacks and sandwiches from 3 p.m. to 7 p.m. Its "bar" serves ice cream, and diversions include foosball, pinball, video games, and, most important, other après-skiers well below the drinking age.

RESTAURANTS

Dining is as varied as skiing and après-ski. In so western a town as Steamboat Springs, El Rancho fills the expectation for a good, moderately priced steak dinner, and the Old West Steakhouse serves beef, elk, buffalo, barbecue, and trout. In a resort like Steamboat, it is also not surprising to find a congenial family restaurant such as the Riverbend Inn, which has steaks and ribs for grownups and pizza and burgers for kids who'll eat nothing but. La Cantina is one of Steamboat's two top Mexican restaurants. The other is Dos Amigos at Ski Time Square.

Less expected are the outstanding seafood restaurants and excellent continental-style places. The freshest fish is at the Coral Grill, a retail restaurant operated by the folks who fly in the town's seafood. The Helm has a good raw bar, and the Steamboat Yacht Club across from Howelson Hill was once a state fish hatchery and now dishes out both good steaks and seafood. The Butcher Shop at Ski Time Square and the Pine Grove, a seventy-five-year-old barn remodeled into a warm eating place, also feature both beef and briny.

The most acclaimed continental fare is served at Cipriani's, an intimate, romantic restaurant in the Sheraton Thunderhead. It features northern Italian classics and creative adaptations. Nearby Mattie Silks is a congenial, candle-lit place brimming with antiques and serving tasty dinners drawn from several European cuisines. Perhaps the best treat is an evening at Hazie's, a table-service, bi-level mountain restaurant in the Thunderhead Lodge. A *prix fixe* dinner, live entertainment in a mellow mode, the lights of the resort, and candles flickering on each table combine into a memorable evening. Beyond the large windows feathery flakes begin to drift down. "Tonight is terrific," the scene seems to say, "and tomorrow will be even better."

Stowe, Vermont

"IF YOU CAN SKI STOWE,
YOU CAN SKI ANYWHERE"

Stowe is one of New England's classic, pretty villages, and Mount Mansfield is one of the country's oldest, most relentlessly challenging, most highly regarded ski mountains. Though they are five miles apart, they are considered as one place, which is widely referred to as the "ski capital of the East." To some this title may seem unwarranted. Nobody ever skied Stowe for the climate, which can be blowy and blizzardy. And Vermont has larger mountains with more runs, more lifts, more snowmaking, more convenient accommodations—especially ones that are warmer and far less rigorous.

But skiers are subjective. They come because, decade after decade, Stowe has offered superlatively challenging skiing, quality lodging, fine food, and a social cachet that dates from the early days of the sport. Stowe is not for dilettantes. It is where socialites go spartan—eschewing high-style skiwear for functional down and queuing up in the chairlift line at an early hour when they'd still be abed at some other resorts.

Stowe was a leading destination ski area until the jet age and was the first true weekend resort within ski-train distance of New York and Boston. Like Sun Valley, Stowe was discovered by the

Stowe has over one hundred miles of cross-country trails, more than any other ski resort.

Mount Mansfield's perpendicular runs and demanding conditions have challenged hardy skiers since 1932.

affluent who helped popularize the sport. It grew quickly and early, and only lost its edge in the seventies when other New England mountains hustled to catch up. It still offers the superior skiing and fine peripherals that continue to attract the tony clientele that was not wooed away by extensive snowmaking and modern lifts, which were late in coming to Stowe.

Mount Mansfield, Vermont's highest mountain, is a humpy ridge with a 4,393-foot summit. To generations of skiers who have tackled its perpendicular runs and endured its demanding conditions, Mansfield is a stern schoolmaster whose requirements are daunting but who is remembered fondly. "If you can ski Stowe, you can ski anywhere" is one of the oldest and truest clichés in skiing.

HISTORY

In 1914, Nathaniel Goodrich, a Dartmouth librarian, made the first documented ski run down the Toll Road, a four-and-a-half mile carriage road to a mountaintop summer hotel called the Summit House. Goodrich, racing a friend descending on snowshoes, barely won. A decade later, Roland Palmedo, a prominent New York skier, who remembered climbing the Toll Road as a youngster, rode to Stowe by train and trolley. He hiked up the old Toll Road on Washington's Birthday 1932 and skied down. After he reported his adventure to New York's Amateur Ski Club, that well-connected group was able to persuade the Civilian Conservation Corps to undertake trail work on Mount Mansfield. The Bruce Trail, the first etched onto the mountain's southeastern face, is no longer skied. But the Nosedive, cut shortly thereafter, with its harrowing Seven Turns at the top, is still one of America's classics.

For seven years, CCC crews, directed by Charlie Lord, Perry Merrill, and Al Gottlieb, were responsible for creating ski trails on mighty Mansfield, touring trails to Luce Hill, and several buildings. The Stowe Ski Club, formed in 1932 and soon renamed the Mount Mansfield Ski Club, was one of the country's earliest and is still a force in developing young ski racers. Three key events occurred in 1936: the first sanctioned downhill was run on the Nosedive; the ski club imported Sepp Ruschp from Austria to teach skiing; and a second-hand rope tow was installed on the newly cleared Toll House Slope at the bottom of the mountain. Snowplows began clearing the road all the way to the bottom of Nosedive, and even the posh Lodge at Smugglers' Notch found it expedient to stay open in winter.

While the locals were laying the foundations for a ski empire, Roland Palmedo and his ASC friends raised $75,000 in Depression dollars to catapult Stowe into the big time with the erection of a single chairlift up Mount Mansfield, the first in the East and the longest, highest one in the country. The Octagon, the landmark day lodge at the top, cost another $15,000. The walk-up era had come to an end.

Then an aristocratic insurance executive named Cornelius Vander Starr took up skiing and complained to Ruschp about the waits for the chairlift, which could be as long as two hours. Together, they hatched a plan for a T-bar on the upper terrain. But it was difficult to get anything done on the mountain, where four companies had ski-related operations: Palmedo's people ran the chairlift; the Mount Mansfield Hotel Company ran the hotel and mountain road; Ruschp had the ski school; and the Burt Lumber Company, which owned 3,000 acres of logged-out land including nearby Spruce Peak, was getting into skiing too. Frustrated by these fragmented operations, Starr consolidated them all in 1948 into one outfit called the Mount Mansfield Company. The next year they finished creating the framework for Stowe by purchasing the luxurious Lodge at Smugglers' Notch. Massive expansions and many refinements followed since the heyday of Lord and Merrill, Palmedo and Starr, but the essence of their mountain remains and gives Stowe its character.

SKIING

In addition to Mansfield, there are easier teaching slopes on Spruce Peak, and a four-passenger gondola was strung up to the saddle between them in 1968. The Toll House Slope was abandoned for a time but has been resuscitated as the location of a condo community. The T-bar on which so many skiers took their first lift ride has been replaced by a chairlift to feed guests directly into the Mount Mansfield runs. The most notable change occurred in 1986-87, when the first high-speed detachable quad in New England replaced the historic single chair and the double which paralleled it. Charlie Lord, a spry octogenarian, took the first ride.

Mansfield and the gondola area have thirty-five trails now, but the most famous and most challenging date from the early days. Mount Mansfield's fabled Front Four—Starr, National, Liftline, and Goat—began as narrow tracks with unforgiving pitches of 35 to 38 degrees. Nosedive is just a hair easier. All five are still unrivaled in their combination of steady pitch and leg-burning length—up to two miles—though selective trail widening (Nosedive's Seven Turns have been pared to four), snowmaking, and grooming have tamed them somewhat.

Mansfield's appeal extends beyond these five trails. Especially since a long triple chairlift replaced the old upper T-bar, the eastern side of the mountain has been a haven for advanced skiers who like challenge but prefer not being blown off the mountain by the ultra-experts who ski the

Front Four run after run. Far easier runs than Standard, Gulch, and North Slope sport black diamonds in southern Vermont, but at Stowe, these are considered intermediate. So are the majority of the Chin runs, a web of sinewy trails served by gondola. It is possible to ski back and forth between the Toll House, across all of Mansfield's terrain, and Chin Clip, covering more distance than trail statistics would indicate.

A car or trolley shuttle is necessary to ski Big Spruce and Little Spruce, adjacent peaks which would constitute a commendable small ski area themselves. With two mild teaching meadows and ten novice-to-intermediate trails, Spruce is the counterweight to intimidating Mount Mansfield. Spruce turns Stowe into a ski resort for all. Home to the ski school which is still run by Sepp Ruschp's son Peter, Little Spruce offers all the warmth and width needed to make new skiers feel comfortable. Though served by one of the oldest chairlifts at Stowe and lacking in snowmaking, Big Spruce offers contrast of another kind, especially when the sun is shining and there's enough natural snow on the ground. The arcs and swales of Big Spruce's three trails—Main Street, Sterling, and Smugglers'—provide skiing in the manner of the early sixties when snowmaking was in its infancy and steep, twisty corridors were giving way to wider, less intimidating runs. Also nearby is Smugglers' Notch, which has long sought an interchangeable lift-ticket arrangement with Stowe to create a European-style ski circus, but "the ski capital of the East" has rejected the offer. (Smugglers', however, does sell a single-ride ticket to returning Stowe skiers.

Stowe is also one of the few New England communities where cross-country skiing matches the attraction of its extensive Alpine facilities. Four touring centers boast a total of over a hundred miles of trails—more than at any other ski resort. Three of the trail systems (Edson Hill Manor, Mount Mansfield Touring Center, and Topnotch-at-Stowe) are interconnected, and three (Edson Hill, Topnotch, and the Trapp Family Lodge) are full resorts with lodging, dining, and après-ski on the premises. All are leading lodges with cross-country as just one of the appeals. Trapps', along with the Woodstock Inn downstate, helped raise cross-country skiing from a kind of counterculture sport into the mainstream.

Mount Mansfield, in a sense, has become a very long tail wagging a very old dog, namely the hamlet of Stowe. The town, which is now so irrevocably linked with skiing, was a land grant from

King George III. It remained a sleepy farm village well into the memory of many of its present residents. "Glossy" has replaced "rural" as one of the operative adjectives, though "charming" and "picturesque" still apply. Downtown Stowe, a cluster of clapboard buildings at the intersection of Routes 100 and 108, has all the elements of New England, except for the obligatory village green. The slender spire of the Congregational church is the sole high-rise in a streetscape composed of a general store, an archetypically quaint country inn, and a cluttered hardware store. This scene is rigorously protected by stringent zoning code enforcement, but Stowe's reality now includes offices of real-estate agents and lawyers, ski shops and art galleries, continental restaurants, and bars with hanging ferns.

The town and ski area are linked by Vermont Route 108, known locally as the Mountain Road—to distinguish it from Route 100, which is Main Street. (In summer, Route 108 winds in a series of tight switchbacks over the pass called Smugglers' Notch. In winter, the Notch isn't plowed, and the road dead-ends at the ski area.) The Mountain Road is the resort's backbone, stacking up with twice-daily traffic jams crawling past a tempting array of lodges, restaurants, and shops—many clustered in mini-malls.

LODGING

The best of Stowe's sixty-odd lodges combine charm, service, and good food, yet a low-key atmosphere prevails. It is not big and brassy but rather charming and comfortable. The Inn at the Mountain, a modern hotel run by the Mount Mansfield Company, is all spaciousness, contemporary luxury, and ski-in, ski-out convenience. Topnotch, once a private club, is now a resort hotel with an elegant atmosphere and sophisticated cuisine. The Green Mountain Inn in the center of town, Edson Hill Manor (where Alan Alda's *Four Seasons* was filmed), Ten Acres Lodge, and The Gables also rate high in quaintness quotient and set great tables besides. There are many casual inns, motels, and motor lodges in various price ranges, the best appointed being the Golden Eagle, the Stoweflake, and the Snowdrift. There's even a huge ski dorm, the Round Hearth, where young skiers stack up in four- to six-bunk rooms, soak amiably in super-size hot tubs, broil by the fire, or compete in video-game prowess.

The Trapp Family Lodge on Luce Hill is nearly as famous as Stowe itself. Trapps' was founded on legend. It was a Vermont farmhouse expanded first to accommodate the huge Trapp family, whose talent was enshrined in *The Sound of Music*. Eventually, the charming chalet that combined the best styles of New England and Austria began taking overnight guests, and now it is a mini-empire dispensing everything from *Wienerschnitzel* in the exquisite restaurant to klister in the touring center's pro shop. Tragically, the antique-filled old inn burned on Christmas Eve 1980 and the elderly Baroness Maria Trapp died in 1987. But the legend and atmosphere live on in a reconstructed lodge. Even those who don't stay at Trapps' normally make a pilgrimage to sample Austrian pastries in the Tea Room.

RESTAURANTS AND APRÈS-SKI

Stowe is a mecca for gourmets no less than for skiers. *Truite avec* some tasty garnish, *pasta á la* trendy, and chateaubriand with a hefty price tag are as easy to find as burgers and brew at other mountains. While Ile de France is Stowe's most acclaimed restaurant, at what other Eastern ski resort does the selection include Scottish haggis (Mr. Pickwick's Pub in Ye Olde England Inne), Transylvanian goulash (Cafe Mozart), sweetbreads in Marsala sauce (Salzburg Inn), or breast of pheasant (Topnotch)?

Après-ski starts with live music at the Mansfield base lodge and eventually oozes down the Mountain Road. The Den and StoweAway are two omni-popular starting points. Charlie B's is elegant, and the Rusty Nail and Sister Kate's are noisy institutions. B.K. Clark's features jazz and rhythm and blues. The Matterhorn is for dancing, and the Last Shot Lounge in the Hayloft for daring games of darts. Beer connoisseurs flock to Mr. Pickwick's. The barkeep taps English, Irish, and American beer and ale from kegs in twenty-ounce mugs. Bottled brews range alphabetically from Aass Bok (Norway) to Tsingtao (China), geographically from the U.S. (thirteen varieties) to Australia (three kinds), and also includes Atlas from Greece and Bresseurs Bière de Paris from France.

Stowe's Winter Carnival, one of the best such events in the East, is normally held the third week in January. Ice sculptures, ski races, skating exhibitions, dogsled races, Las Vegas night, Tyrolean night, fireworks, and snow golf (using colored balls) are among the highlights.

Whatever the week, whatever the season, Stowe and Mount Mansfield are perennial highlights of the skiing life. They always require something extra of skiers: a little more time to reach, a little more money to stay and dine, and a little more skill to ski. But for everything it gets, Stowe gives too: the stately beauty of northern Vermont, first-rate facilities on and off the mountain, and first-rate skiing, which still ranks among the best in the East.

Sugarloaf, Maine

SUGARLOAFERS ARE KNOWN
FOR SWEEPING GIANT SLALOM
TURNS DOWN FALL-LINE RUNS
OF GENEROUS WIDTH

Sugarloaf is unique in eastern skiing. This free-standing mountain, Maine's second highest peak, dominates the landscape much as an ocean liner dominates the seas around it. When Per Lindstrand and Richard Branson embarked on their historic transatlantic hot-air balloon voyage in July 1987, they took off from Sugarloaf's 4,237-foot summit. That's high enough for fifty acres of above-the-timberline snowfields, the only such lift-served terrain in the East. Skiing them is a New England springtime ritual, but they are just the crowning glory of a mountain that is exceptional both in demanding terrain and in sheer size.

Several years ago, a sturdy local skier named Tom Hildreth rode every lift and skied every run (what then amounted to 65,000 vertical feet) in a single day. By the spring of 1987, when the trails had increased to fifty-six, he could no longer accomplish this feat. With two lifts and four trails added in 1988-89, skiing it all in one day will forever remain impossible—unless Sugarloaf puts in night skiing or switches to all high-speed lifts.

Sugarloaf was founded as an experts' mountain, and even though it now has delightful, far easier terrain and a compact slopeside village, it has retained that image. The new facilities have turned

The Loaf from a day and weekend area, for fussy Mainiacs and Bostonians, into a legitimate vacation destination, but its reputation as one of the East's toughest ski mountains remains.

Sugarloaf's pleasant Village creates an aura of cozy intimacy that complements the monolithic mountain. The mountain says, "Ski me if you can," yet the Village stands as a warm oasis of fun and friendliness, light and laughter amid the forbidding woods and quiet fields of south central Maine. While Vermont and New Hampshire attract skiers from the Middle Atlantic states and southern New England who dilute the real Yankee atmosphere, Sugarloaf's primary draw is from Massachusetts on north. Therefore, though the architecture is a contemporary mix of warm red brick, warmer natural wood, and lots of glass, the atmosphere maintains a large measure of the indefinable quality the natives call "down home," which translates roughly as "old-fashioned New England."

SKIING

When Olympic gold medal-winning marathoner Joan Benoit Samuelson or Boston Celtics great John Havlicek ski, it is usually "down home" at Sugarloaf. But the greatest testimonial is not from celebrity endorsements but from regular skiers who prefer it even to mountains that are easier to reach—and to ski. Sugarloaf's percentage of really good skiers is exceptional—the peer of Cannon Mountain and Stowe. Yet The Loaf's regulars are a breed apart. While the skiers at those other great eastern mountains specialize in the tight, controlled turns required to survive on steep, narrow trails, Sugarloafers are known for sweeping giant slalom turns down fall-line runs of generous width. The mountain used to breed mean mogul skiers, too, but since it has embarked on an extensive grooming program, even the bumpers have also learned to love high-speed GS turns.

One gondola (a blessing on the bone-chilling days that can be expected in northern New England), two new fixed-grip quad chairs, one triple, seven doubles, four T-bars, and one beginner tow spread the skiers all over the sprawling mountain, from the expanded East Side steeps to the gentle, isolated roads on the western part. The latter include long, sheltered wanderers like West Mountain Road, Glancer, and Windrow that make Sugarloaf a commendable area for novice skiers. Bullwinkle's

*The Loaf has an experts-only reputation,
but there are novice trails too.*

Grill, a warm log cabin near the top of the West Mountain and Windrow chairs, is a popular hot chocolate stop for chilled children—and their parents. When spring finally comes to Maine, it has a great outdoor deck, too.

Skiers need not go as far north as Sugarloaf for their fun, but those who treasure the steeps that shoot straight off the windswept summit make the trip because they want to. They have the choice of routes to the top. One way is via the four-passenger gondola. To ride it all day, however, requires constant top-to-bottom skiing, including easier terrain near the base, and a lot of waiting in line, but it's a bonanza when the windchill factor is low. But Sugarloaf regulars are a hardy bunch who didn't get to ski so well by standing in line. Anxious, in the typical Yankee way, to get in the most skiing for their money, they bundle up and take the Double Runner East chair to the Spillway East chair and ski the upper mountain all day.

Many stick to the runs closest to Spillway—those treacherous steeps like Narrow Gauge, Skidder, Double Bitter, or Competition Hill. Before Sugarloaf acquired its fleet of Kässbohrer groomers, and even now when the slopes are groomed, they are demanding. As soon as you get a head of steam going, the snow may disappear under your skis and the trail turn into an icy waterfall. You crank in those edges—you did have them sharpened, didn't you?—until the hairiest part is passed. Visiting skiers tend to slow down; Sugarloaf regulars don't.

New Englanders, with an in-bred tolerance for the spartan, happily use the uncrowded King Pine T-bar to ski the eastern runs. Marked black like those off the Spillway chair, they are nevertheless somewhat milder—charcoal gray, perhaps—thanks to diligent trail work. These runs have a good steady pitch but with fewer harrowing drop-offs. Recognizing the need for more upper-intermediate and advanced terrain, Sugarloaf has put in one quad lift and four upper-mountain trails to expand this East Side sector. (The other quad heads up the eastern side from the base.)

Strong skiers should take part in the unique Ski With Management program at seven-thirty on Sunday mornings, just after the Patrol but before the lifts open to the general public. Where else can you get the ear of a top area executive during a lift ride and ski so huge a mountain with just a handful of other hardy souls? Even when you wait for normal skiing hours, Sugarloaf is a special place, with a skiing experience apart from any other eastern mountain. Its combination of remoteness and spaciousness exists nowhere else in the region. The amazing thing is that, for a few scary months, the skiing world feared that Sugarloaf would close down.

HISTORY

In 1950, Amos Winter, a general store manager in Kingfield, sixteen miles away, led a group of locals who were tired of traveling to New Hampshire and Vermont for challenging skiing. They figured there must be acceptably steep terrain somewhere in the mountains of the Rangeley Lakes area. They first found an old fire trail to the summit of Bigelow Mountain, which indeed had the slopes they sought, but Central Maine Power soon made it inaccessible by damming up a nearby lake. The group, by then known as the Bigelow Boys, turned to Sugarloaf, where they found steep upper runs and those splendid snowfields. Assured that this was indeed the place, they engaged pioneering trail designer Sel Hannah to lay out the first run. Volunteers from the newly formed Sugarloaf Ski Club cut Winter's Way, a twisting high-mountain run which is still skied, and built a rope tow, a warming hut at the base, and a lean-to at the top. New lifts and trails were added as club members could afford. In 1955, after local investors turned it from a club into a publicly held corporation, the burgeoning ski area financed three more lifts, four trails, and a real base lodge. The 9,000-foot-long gondola came in 1966.

During the seventies, as skiing boomed, Sugarloaf began making its mark as a weekend area with destination resort potential. The area hosted a World Cup downhill in 1973 to spread its name around, but real estate development was thought to be the quickest route to future growth. Twenty-one slopeside condominium units, the first in Maine, were built and the Village Center with shops and restaurants also took shape. It was a daring move for conservative and frugal Yankees. The need for snowmaking hit home during the snow drought of 1973-74, and the following year pipes were run up Narrow Gauge, then the world's highest snowmaking system. But it was a case of too little, too late.

Covering one top-to-bottom run doth not a major system make, and Sugarloaf's snowmaking continued to lag behind the giants who had a head start on assuring reliable water supplies and had earlier laid the groundwork for high-powered snowmaking operations. By the mid-eighties, The Loaf was in trouble. Having invested so much in real estate without reliable snow to attract condo buyers or renters, Maine's main mountain was in trouble. Trouble was spelled C-H-A-P-T-E-R E-L-E-V-E-N.

When the Sugarloaf Mountain Corporation fell under the Federal Bankruptcy Court's protection in 1986, the chairman of the board said, "Snowmaking is our first priority, and there is no second." The reorganized company emerged from Chapter 11 fourteen months later with a $2-million commitment to nearly quadruple snowmaking capacity to cover 75 percent of the sprawling terrain. Additional grooming equipment, expanded base and rental facilities, a new children's center, and new lifts and runs soon followed.

LODGING

In its ski club days, Sugarloaf had one on-mountain overnight facility, a sixteen-by-twenty-foot cabin with a women's bunkroom on one end and a men's on the other. It wasn't much in the way of luxury, but it was warm and the price was just $1.00 a night for members and $1.50 for guests. And you had to bring your own blanket. The resort is one of the few major ones that still has a dorm, a large log house called the Sugarloafer's Ski Dorm, just off Route 27, the main north-south highway. MAP lodging now skims the $20 mark, but there is still the option to save a few dollars by bringing your own linens.

The resort also, and predictably, offers luxury lodging. The base area is peppered with six hundred attractive condominiums, but its most notable accommodation is the Sugarloaf Mountain Hotel. Sprawled across the base area, steps from the Village, lifts, and base lodge, the attractive brick hotel topped by steep gables features exceptionally spacious rooms. Nearby, at the base of the newly expanded beginner slope is the venerable Sugarloaf Inn.

Other lodging is found along Route 27, and Sugarloaf skiers do rest their heads as far afield as Kingfield and Farmington to the south and Stratton and Rangeley to the north. Two of the best of the off-campus choices are in Kingfield. The Inn on Winter's Hill is a splendid hilltop mansion designed by the Stanley Brothers (best known for developing the Stanley Steamer) for a wealthy local merchant. Now on the National Register of Historic Places, it offers romantic Victorian rooms and dining in Le Papillon, which serves French specialties as exquisite as the decor. The nearby Herbert Inn has simpler rooms but more complicated cuisine in the new French style.

RESTAURANTS

One Stanley Avenue, also a National Register property, was the home of a Kingfield lumber magnate. It now serves exceptionally well-prepared New England specialties, also in a setting of Victorian opulence. (Next door is a small inn under the same management.) But it isn't necessary to travel all the way to Kingfield for fine food. In the Village, it is available at the Truffle Hound, a pleasantly ambitious establishment; at Arabella's, a contemporary restaurant in the Sugarloaf Mountain Hotel; and at Gladstone's at slopeside. All offer quality selections from various continental cuisines. The Seasons, a pleasant greenhouse restaurant at the Sugarloaf Inn, has moderately priced dinners, especially steak and seafood offerings, and an excellent salad bar.

Still, casual dining prevails at the resort. Gepetto's kitchen starts with light breakfast, segues into casual lunches, and keeps cooking until the last dinner has been served around nine-thirty in the evening. Pinocchio's, its downstairs component, is popular with youngsters who enjoy pizza, soft drinks, ice cream, and video games. The Gladstone's glassed-in dining room is a pleasant dinner setting, but at lunch it's a real treat when it's warm enough for a barbecue on the slopeside outdoor deck. Hug's, half a mile from the resort on Route 27, is a cozy red, green, and white hut serving Italian fare, while the super-casual Mountain Lodge in Carrabassett Valley has two restaurants, Macho's serving Mexican specialties and Der Weinkeller for German dishes.

APRÈS-SKI

The Bag's busy bar has a lively atmosphere, a menu of terrific munchies and light meals, and either sports action on a big-screen TV or live entertainment. The Widowmaker Lounge and Maxwell's, both on the upper level of the expanded base lodge, also offer live entertainment. It's unthinkable that one could drive by Judson's on Route 27 and not notice the place. Its blue neon mountainscape is a beacon to northbound skiers as they are approaching Sugarloaf, and its Gondola Bar is a top after-ski watering hole. Farther down the road is Tufulio's, a lively saloon that also offers modestly priced Italian food.

OTHER ACTIVITIES

With eighty-five groomed trails, the Carrabassett Valley Ski Touring Center is Maine's largest. It offers all levels of terrain, a warm and spacious lodge, and skating on an Olympic-size rink. The Sugartree Health Club's outstanding facilities include pool, hot tubs, racquetball courts, and exercise and fitness equipment and programs.

Sugarloaf is a compelling mountain coupled with a warm, cozy village. It's an incomparable ski resort that those hardcore skiers who know it choose above all others.

Sun Valley, Idaho

WITH A CLUBBINESS UNMATCHED
THIS SIDE OF GSTAAD OR ST. MORITZ,
SUN VALLEY HAS ONE OF THE BIGGEST
AND BEST MOUNTAINS IN AMERICA

Sun Valley is skiing on a fantastic mountain, in a world-class vacation community, and living in the brilliantly created resort that effectively launched skiing as we know it. More than fifty years ago, skiers began arriving in this snowy basin near Ketchum, the remote and rugged sheep-ranching Idaho town where Ernest Hemingway made his last home. They first came at the behest of W. Averell Harriman, an enthusiastic skier and president of the Union Pacific Railroad, who, wishing to give people a reason to ride his rails in winter, had dispatched an Austrian aristocrat named Count Felix Schaffgotsch to find the best locale for a new ski resort. After the resort was built, Harriman hired Steve Hannagan, an indefatigable promoter, who put Sun Valley on the map that movie stars and socialites used to plan their pleasures.

Sun Valley was the site of the world's first chairlift, the country's first built-for-skiing luxury hotel, and its first mountain restaurant. As the world's first resort developed for skiing, it was a place where a generation of Hollywood starlets frolicked with a generation of Austrian ski instructors, where Sonja Henie danced with John Payne in *Sun Valley Serenade*, and where Eddie Duchin's

Bald Mountain (with Ketchum at its base and the Sun Valley resort in the foreground) boasts some of the most extraordinary ski terrain in the country.

music set the tone for a sophisticated, scintillating après-ski life. Over the years, Sun Valley has remained right with the right crowd—even after Union Pacific sold it in 1964 to William Janss, a real estate developer, and again after Janss sold it to Salt Lake City hotel and oil baron Earl Holding in 1977. Each change elicited fears from the loyal legions, but while Sun Valley has had its ups and downs, its ups have been stratospheric and its downs have not been so bad. Sun Valley is too isolated, too big, simply too special to spoil.

The resort's enduring clubbiness is unmatched this side of Gstaad or St. Moritz. When Sun Valley celebrated its fiftieth anniversary in January 1986, the biggest names in skiing and many show business luminaries congregated there again in a larger-than-life rerun of its glamorous heyday. Instead of Claudette Colbert, Madeleine Carroll, and Errol Flynn supplying the luster, for the fiftieth it was Brooke Shields and George Hamilton, Mary Lou Retton and Dr. Ruth, Cathy Lee Crosby and Jamie Lee Curtis, plus fabled racers from many nations and all generations who mingled on and off the slopes. It was, in short, the ordinary Sun Valley mix, in extraordinary concentration, celebrating what, in effect, was the demi-centennial of skiing in America.

*Sun Valley
sun worshippers.*

SKIING

Sun Valley is wealth and history and tradition, but it's also great skiing. It has to be, for the resort is remote, and snow conditions and weather can be iffy. In recent years, cover at Christmas has often been thin, and January, when the powder is best, can be so cold that the name Sun Valley—invoking a powerful image of fair skies and warm rays—proves to be one of Hannagan's public relations masterstrokes.

Yet Sun Valley boasts some of the most extraordinary ski terrain in the country, and both the skiing and the lifestyle owe as much to the European as to the American. Thousands of skiers have nostalgic thoughts of learning to ski on Dollar Mountain, a beginner's paradise which prepares new skiers for truly big mountains. But when people say they have skied Sun Valley, they really mean Bald Mountain—at 3,400 vertical feet, one of the biggest of them all. It is composed of three rounded peaks strung along a vast *massif*. In Alpine fashion, chairlifts rise this way and that, and the terrain cants toward almost all compass directions—a wonderful anomaly in American

The first ski school of Austrians arrived in 1936.

skiing. The immensity is magnified because there are few trees and hardly any lift lines. With the addition of three new high-speed quad chairs, Sun Valley has the best ratio of lift capacity to beds of any major American resort—over 25,000 skiers an hour on the lifts against fewer than 10,000 pillows. More astonishingly, on the average day—meaning not at Christmas or President's Weekend—there are usually only about 3,500 skiers on this mega-mountain.

Whether a skier prefers the expansiveness of the bowls or the maxi-challenge of the fabled mogul runs, whether he gravitates to the groomed or escapes to the powder, the single most compelling characteristic is the straight-down nature of the skiing on an uncompromised mountain that provides lots of elbow room but little relief. The runs may be wide, but they are also long and relentless, each one demanding a measure more of energy and consistent skiing than the symbol on the trail map would indicate.

The most popular entry into Baldy's vast domain is from the Warm Springs side. The chairs cruise over a progression of wide, fir-lined runs, when suddenly the treeline demarcates the boundary between forest and mountaintop. Soon Baldy's 9,150-foot summit is in view, looking like a corner of the Alps. From it, as far as the eye can see, there is a vista of sweeping bowls and strings of chairlifts. In the clear air, perception is so skewed that it is difficult to determine whether distance is to be measured in feet or miles. How far are the Christmas and Ridge chairs? Is the Lookout chair almost horizontal? It links the main Baldy summit with a second peak.

The initial impulse is to plunge right into the nearest of Baldy's seven side-by-side bowls, Christmas Bowl. Newcomers approach it cockily, but once they ski to the edge, and their hearts stand still before this steep-walled gully which cannot possibly be a blue square, which is how it is marked on the map, the urge to plunge in, for many skiers, passes. They may continue to the next bowl, hoping it will be easier (it is, a little). Others breathe deeply and traverse tentatively into the broad-beamed ravine that looms all the larger when there is no way out except down. Once the commitment has been made, however, the pleasure does begin and dread turns into delight. The bowls are addictive, and, in fact, they are easier as one progresses toward the horizon. Easter, Lookout, Lefty, Mayday, Far Out, and Siggi's are the main ones—each somewhat different, each quite divine. They are awesome on stormy days when the snow falls more quickly than it can be skied off, and even more challenging when the snow has been packed. Late in the season, they sprout impressive mogul fields.

The other entry to Baldy (and more practical for residents of downtown Ketchum) is via River Run. It provides the quickest access to Seattle Ridge, a complex of relatively easy high-mountain runs that snare the best morning light. This sprawling peak, with a web of green and blue runs served by the Cold Springs and Seattle Ridge chairs, is also the beneficiary of the most assiduous application of Sun Valley's renowned slope-grooming efforts. The powder that is left largely ungroomed in the bowls is here manipulated into white velvet. Experts warm up on these runs, and many recreational skiers use them as an all-day playground. Here Sun Valley has honored its most illustrious skiing daughters with trails named Gretchen's Gold after Gretchen Fraser, the 1948 Olympic slalom champion, and Christin's Silver for Christin Cooper, the 1984 giant slalom runner-up.

Those who do not dive into the powdery offerings of Baldy's bowls or cruise the slopes of Cold Springs and Seattle Ridge usually are hot skiers who prefer the mogul runs off the mountain's long central ridge. Baldy's bumps, in many experts' minds, are the best of all. Exhibition, a run that packs the quadruple whammy of super steepness, significant sidehill, mammoth moguls, and maximum visibility (because almost its entire length is visible from the chairlift) is arguably the most famous bump run in America. Nearly as savage are Upper Olympic, which is both shorter and less visible, and Holiday, challenging because its sidehill is more wicked than Exhibition's.

At the end of the day, the crowd moves to the long, lush Warm Springs runs, whose consistent pitches are interrupted only by the cat tracks that enable skiers to mix easier slopes with steeper ones as energy and inclination dictate. Warm Springs is the best end-of-the-day skiing in the country. In winter, the top après-ski spots at the base are crowded, cozy oases of merriment. In spring, the action moves outdoors onto decks.

LODGING

It is luxury and service, even more than tradition, which still sets Sun Valley apart from all other resorts. To drive under the portico of the Sun Valley Lodge is to motor into the past. To enter is to step through into a pampering world that is steeped in modern cultural history. Photographs of the rich and famous who skied there line the hallways of the place where Ernest Hemingway completed the manuscript of *For Whom the Bell Tolls* (in Room 206). After some years of neglect, the Lodge was renovated for the fiftieth, and it is once again classy as well as classic. The public rooms are casual yet elegant. Music wafting from the Duchin Room is Cole Porterish pop or classic jazz. In the Lodge's spacious dining room, guests are lulled by soft music, soft candlelight, and the soft touch of attentive white-gloved waiters. There's not much that could be worth missing a day on Baldy for, but when dinner reservations are impossible to obtain, skip a few hours on the mountain and try Sunday brunch.

The Sun Valley Inn, originally built as a less expensive alternative to the Lodge, also has been redone. In the Inn's case, this involved an upgrading rather than a refurbishing, so that such luxury touches as marble bathrooms co-exist with more practical features, including a cafeteria where youngsters can eat while their parents are dining at the Lodge. These two highly original and highly famous hotels flank the Sun Valley Mall (a double line of shops and eating places) and the fabled outdoor ice rink where Sonja Henie enchanted the world with her spins, leaps, and dimples. Nearby is a gaggle of luxurious private homes and condominiums.

Not far away is Elkhorn, a modern condo community that nestles against the backside of Dollar Mountain. Down valley is Ketchum, a spruced-up ranching town which combines western rusticity with high-fashion glitz and offers the resort's most interesting restaurants, most raucous nightspots, most eclectic shopping, and most varied accommodations, including moderately priced lodges and motels and even condo complexes pocketed along the back streets. Commodious condominiums may also be found at Warm Springs, a mini-village that is conveniently located next to the lifts. Million-dollar homes are north of Ketchum, and also off Fairway Road and Elkhorn Road.

RESTAURANTS

While a sleighride to dinner at rustic Trail Creek Cabin is a must, there are many conventional dining choices along the Sun Valley Mall and in Ketchum. In the Mall, the Konditorei is for light meals and heavy desserts; the Ore House serves steaks and seafood; and the Ram is a notable purveyor of wild game. Desperado's and the Bald Mountain Cantina in Ketchum and Tequila Joe's in Elkhorn spice a cold winter's night Mexicanically. A Matter of Taste in Trail Creek Village is an intimate boutique restaurant specializing in fine pastas. Elsewhere in Ketchum, Soupçon has splendid adaptations of continental and American specialties, while the highly acclaimed Evergreen also presents a contemporary mix of cuisines. The Christiania is famous for fine continental fare, while Chez Michel (owned and operated by the former head coach of the women's U.S. Ski Team) serves an authentic and delectable French cuisine. Freddie's specializes in the hearty specialties of the Alsace, while the Warm Springs Ranch is the best all-around place for a beautiful setting, warm ambiance, and wonderful American food, and ever popular with locals is the Pioneer, a long-time prime-rib specialist.

APRÈS-SKI

The first stop, at the Creekside or Barsotti's Mountain Cafe at the base of the Warm Springs lifts, is to bend an elbow and see who's around. The second is most likely at the Ram Bar in the Sun Valley Mall, where country and rock inject a lively note into the otherwise sedate atmosphere. Because Sun Valley is a bastion of the traditional ski week, private lesson-takers, and their suave instructors, also abound. Then everyone hits the pool.

A night on the town is a counterpoint to the elegance of the Lodge, when the town is Ketchum. The younger crowd flocks to Slavey's and Whiskey Jacques' (pronounced "Whiskey Jack's") for jumping music and filling grub at relatively modest prices. Joe Cannon, a bawdy singer as closely associated with Sun Valley as Don Ho is with Honolulu, can be found in one of the resort's major nightspots, while the Duchin Room's eminently danceable pop music appeals to a more sedate crowd. Both are don't-miss experiences.

OTHER ACTIVITIES

Sun Valley's appeals go far beyond the extraordinary Alpine skiing and sparkling nightlife. Its cross-country skiing is also exceptional. Several touring centers offer trail systems as meticulously groomed as the best mountain runs. The Sun Valley Nordic Touring Center, now under the aegis of the mountain company, offers civilized lunch and dinner tours to Trail Creek Cabin, and several trekking companies organize more rugged guided trips into the outback, including one which specializes in overnighters with accommodations in Mongolian-style yurts—a far cry from the luxury and super service of the Sun Valley Lodge and Inn.

The Lodge's huge, steaming outdoor hot pool—another Sun Valley first—is an après-ski must, while the Sun Valley Athletic Club, located in Ketchum, is a treat for those who find relaxation in pumping iron. Skating at the Lodge's outdoor rink, under the eyes of patrons of the dining room, draws daily crowds and is a wonderful activity for youngsters. Next to the rink is a hockey arena where the Sun Valley Suns battle fiercely against other semi-pro teams on Friday evenings.

Ketchum may be the only resort where the library is a major tourist attraction. Immense and handsome, the privately financed community library keeps log fires roaring in a huge stone fireplace. It is ultimately relaxing to sink into a deep-cushioned armchair and let your gaze wander to the floor-to-vaulted-ceiling windows which face Baldy.

Sun Valley is like an old friend, and with half-a-century of history and great skiing, it is comforting to know that Sun Valley, the first, is still among the best ski resorts in North America.

Taos, New Mexico

TAOS IS A PLACE WHERE ORDINARY PEOPLE BECOME EXTRAORDINARY SKIERS

Few ski areas are as much a reflection of one man as Taos Ski Valley is of founding father Ernie Blake. The resort, a huddle of intimate lodges nestled amid the soaring Sangre de Cristo Mountains of northern New Mexico, combines European ambiance with western American snow. It is, as its creator envisioned it thirty-five years ago, a congenial haven that attracts skiing's most ardent aficionados, not because it is big, not because it is brassy, and certainly not because it is convenient—for it is none of these—but simply because it is one of the best.

Taos is a place where ordinary people become extraordinary skiers. It is a jewel where lodging is civilized and dining memorable, where nightlife is mild, and where the traditional ski week still prevails. It has a European pattern woven into the Hispanic-Indian tapestry of the Southwest. Less than twenty miles away are the Taos Pueblo, America's oldest continuously inhabited community, and the town of Taos, an historic Spanish colonial outpost and today an important art colony.

The tale of the Taos ski resort has more than a bit of kismet, the fulfillment of an elusive dream of one of skiing's visionaries. From the outset, Ernie Blake, a *skimeister* in his native Switzerland, knew what his ideal ski resort was. It just took him a while to find it. In the years before America

Taos combines an intimate atmosphere and terrific skiing.

entered World War II, Blake was one of the first generation of Europeans who crossed the Atlantic to pioneer a skiing way of life.

Ernie was employed by Saks Fifth Avenue, selling skis and teaching skiing, at a time when there were just two western towns with powder and promise: Sun Valley and Aspen. As Blake and his New York-born fiancée Rhoda were driving west to check them out, she confessed she would eventually like to live in New Mexico "if we can afford it and if we survive the war."

Survive they did. Blake, who served as a U.S. Army intelligence officer and eventually as an interrogator of German officers and atomic scientists, returned to the mountains after the war. He commuted between two jobs, one managing the Santa Fe Basin ski area and one running a now-defunct ski area near Glenwood Springs, Colorado. Bored with flying his Cessna in a straight line, Ernie began taking detours, always searching for the perfect mountain, one with a potential vertical of around 3,000 feet, excellent snow and a pleasant climate. In 1953, he discovered the soaring 11,000 footers near Twining, New Mexico, an abandoned copper mining town. The mountains were steep, and the valleys tight, yet the snow looked wonderful.

The following winter, Blake climbed those mountains in three-and-a-half feet of fresh powder and was convinced that his airborne instincts had been right. He moved his family, which by then included three young children, to a place even his ski-savvy friends felt had no future. But the Blakes had faith in their dream, and they put in the hard work and time to make it come true. They began laying out the terrain by skiing the densely wooded steeps and daubing paint on trees to mark trails to be cut.

When Taos Ski Valley opened in 1955, the Blakes were a bit like the Swiss Family Robinson, living in a nineteen-foot house trailer which served as both home and business office, where he improvised every aspect of the ski area's design, construction, and management. Michael Blake, then an eleven-year-old who could barely see over the vehicle's dashboard, supplemented early lift service by driving Taos's single snowcat, towing powder-hungry skiers in his wake. The family would sell tickets until nine-thirty and then go skiing. Anyone who arrived after that would hoist a flag, and the next Blake down the mountain would make the ticket sale. There couldn't have been too many interruptions, for Taos's gross revenues that first winter were just $1,600.

Expansion came slowly. The first solid building was the Hondo Lodge, a stone bastion named for a rushing mountain creek that was the resort's first water source. The Hondo provided the Blakes with a small apartment and skiers with the first slopeside lodging. The following year, a young French ski racer named Jean Mayer arrived to manage the Hondo and to become Taos's first ski school director. He was soon joined by his kid brother Dadou, who was such a cocky youngster that Ernie fired him. Dadou, chastened, later returned and today the Mayer brothers operate the St. Bernard and the Edelweiss, which were the next lodges to be built at the base of Taos and are still the most acclaimed. Today there are two more lodges, the Thunderbird and the Innsbruck, a couple of modest condominium developments, a sprinkling of chalets off in the woods, and a few shops. And that's it.

In 1972 the access road was paved (the roads in the resort itself still aren't), and the following year the ski area finally began turning a profit. The Blake family is still fully involved. Ernie and Rhoda live in an apartment atop the base lodge where they can, and do, keep an eye on things. Ernie has slowed down a bit, but he is still intensely active, as evidenced by his daily presence at ski school lineup, his ever-crackling two-way radio, and his constantly ringing telephone. He personally interviews all prospective employees and makes even minute decisions on resort operations.

Son Michael is the mountain manager. After all, he grew up tinkering with ski lifts and snowcats the way a farmer's son fiddles with tractors and plows. Daughter Wendy runs the ski shop, one of her mother's original tasks. Chris Stagg came in 1969 from upstate New York to teach skiing, eventually married the boss's daughter, and is now the resort's marketing director and ski school supervisor. Peter, the baby of the Blake family, is a top instructor. So is Chris's brother Berkeley, who taught Jimmy and Rosalynn Carter how to ski.

The former First Couple are just two of the many non-skiers who have become skiers, novices who have become intermediates, and advanced skiers who have become true experts under the tutelage of the elite Taos Ski School, which now numbers nearly one hundred instructors. Until the access road was paved, Taos was practical only for those able to stay once they got there. And since there was little else to do in the isolated valley—no ice skating, no swimming, little cross-country skiing, minimal shopping—and since the lessons were included in the package plans at the lodges, even people who normally eschew instruction went into ski school.

If anyone had done a business analysis on what makes a ski resort succeed, Taos would never have been built. Conventional wisdom has it that its terrain is too steep for the mass market, its valley is too confining to support a real resort, its trail layout too awkward, its potential for après-ski and non-ski activities too limited, and its access from major population centers too difficult. In reality, Taos has the highest return rate of any major American ski resort, and the percentage of guests in ski school is the greatest on this side of the Atlantic. To this day, even with more vacationers overnighting in the town of Taos and with the addition of day skiers from Santa Fe and Albuquerque, the traditional ski week predominates, with small classes—seven students maximum—honing their technique all over the mountain.

Much of the allure of the Taos ski week comes from a genuine friendliness and enthusiasm radiating from every employee (Ernie will dump anyone who doesn't exhibit these qualities), and much comes from the high-caliber instructors and from students who could themselves be teaching on any other mountain. But the rest of Taos's appeal lies in breathtaking steeps, hidden bowls, and powder chutes spread across the mountain.

SKIING

Skiers arriving at night are awestruck by Taos at morning light. Number One lift, the original chair, and Number Five, running parallel with it, seem to go straight up the mountain. Are these lifts or are these elevators? They must be lifts, for beneath them is a ribbon of white punctuated with monster moguls. The trail, legendary Al's Run, is so intimidating that Ernie was prompted to post a large sign stating: "Don't panic. You're looking at only 1/90th of Taos Ski Valley. We have many easy runs too!" Indeed, Taos has some mild slopes suitable for novices and intermediates, but since 80 percent of Taos's guests ski parallel or better and 50 percent are capable of handling the steepest runs, the black and double-black diamonds have great appeal.

Al's isn't the longest run at Taos (that is a tame five-and-a-half-miler called Rubezahl) nor the steepest (that honor goes to Stauffenberg, with a hairy 37-degree pitch), but it is the most awesome because it is the most obvious. Elsewhere, the chicken traverse or the emergency stem turn can be executed in secret, but riders on two lifts bear witness to any bailout on Al's.

With massive moguls and 1,800 vertical feet of sustained pitch, Al's and the other north-facing runs on the lower mountain are at their best in the early afternoon sunshine. First thing in the morning, Taos veterans opt for the high country, reached by another pair of parallel lifts, Numbers Two and Six, also known as Chief and Superchief. They unload on a high plateau where the resort's three avalanche-rescue dogs cavort. This plateau unleashes Taos's staggering options of expert terrain.

Off to the right is the West Basin Ridge, a hike along a high traverse. To the left is Highline Ridge, a hike off in the other direction. And beyond is Tresckow Ridge and the farthest reaches of skiable terrain. Anyone who wants to ski these ridges has to sign out with the Ski Patrol. The terrain is spectacular by any measure—steep cornices followed by vertiginous chutes feeding into runouts that spell R-E-L-I-E-F to all but the sturdiest skiers.

The West Basin chutes—Stauffenberg, Zdarsky, and a trio named for the three oldest Taos lodges—are narrower. The wider ones off Highline—Niños Heroes, Juarez, and Hidalgo—are more like steep gullies than out-and-out chutes but they are also relentless and demanding. Twin Trees Chute, Corner Chute, and Tresckow, all off Tresckow Ridge, are awe-inspiring glades.

Another option, which provides extreme skiing without hiking and without cornices, is to take the green-circle run called Bambi and drop off into Walkyries Chute, Sir Arnold Lunn, Lorelei, or Longhorn. There are dizzying drops, tricky glades, and astonishing powder pockets even long after a storm. Except for Longhorn, all these runs end up at the bottom of Number Seven chair, Taos's newest and its only triple. This lift accesses a handful of trails carved as a concession to those seeking less taxing terrain. The liftline run is Maxie's, named after the late balloonist Maxie Anderson, a Taos regular.

Looming beyond Tresckow Ridge is Kachina Peak, topping out at 12,481 feet. This topographic landmark is to Taos what the Matterhorn is to Zermatt or Mont Blanc is to Chamonix. The peak itself is usually skiable from mid-January, and is not too difficult by Taos standards.

Kachina Bowl, which hunkers in a cirque near the treeline, is joyfully skiable. The upper terrain consists of two open bowls, Hunziker and Shalako, one on each side of the Kachina chairlift. These are designated with blue squares, but on other mountains, they'd easily be blacks. These bowls are wonderful for beginning powder skiers, for Ernie Blake contends that it is impossible to learn to ski powder anywhere but on steep terrain. The Kachina bowls prove Ernie's point. Kachina's lower runs merge, zigzag, and cross one another in a happy hodgepodge. Blue squares prevail.

RESTAURANTS, APRÈS-SKI, AND OTHER ACTIVITIES

The Phoenix Restaurant nestles at the base of the Kachina runs, and some condo-dwellers and day skiers indeed have lunch there, but toward noon, most Taos skiers migrate down the long traverse known as Home Run, back into the valley. Lodge packages include three meals a day.

When the weather is sunny, as it so often is, the choicest lunch spot is the broad terrace of the St. Bernard's Rathskeller. If there weren't a snow fence to protect diners from the occasional runaway ski, it would literally be possible to ski to the table. La Bodega in the Hondo is cozy on snowy days and specializes in fiery chili and stuffed baked potatoes.

The Edelweiss serves only breakfast (its guests dine at the St. Bernard), but the other lodges put on three lavish meals a day. The St. Bernard has frequently been singled out as one of skidom's

Each day a Mexican glass decanter (porron) filled with martinis is hidden by an instructor. Students are expected to find it.

best restaurants. It is astonishing that Jean Mayer, after a full day on the slopes, contrives to present the night's menu to as many as 140 guests seated at long tables designed for conviviality—and Mayer serves many of the dishes himself.

Nightlife is minimal, and after a day's hard skiing, most people happily turn in long before the clock strikes twelve. A few beers, stories swapped by the fireside, perhaps jazz at the Thunderbird, a bit of dancing at the St. Bernard, or a drink at the Edelweiss—and that's it.

Most vacationers spend at least one evening down canyon amid the bright lights of Taos proper. The shops stay open a couple of nights a week, and there is complimentary bus transportation between town and ski resort. It's almost like astral projection to travel so quickly from the snow and fir trees of the resort to the desert and adobe of the town. But there abound art galleries, trendy restaurants, lively bars, and shops purveying Indian crafts, turquoise jewelry, and stylish fashions.

LODGING

For people who find the resort too confining, or for those who book too late to get a reservation, a rental car and a room in town provide an alternative. The historic Taos Inn, a landmark in the center of town, is a romantic place. Each antique-filled room has a wood-burning fireplace and hand-loomed Indian rugs and bedspreads, and the hotel's Adobe Bar is a popular gathering spot for locals and tourists alike. The Quail Ridge Inn, along the access road, is a sizable and well-appointed complex reasonably convenient to town and ski area.

Still, for most skiers, the first choice is one of the Taos Ski Valley lodges. The rooms may be simple compared to newer, more studiously luxurious resorts, but nowhere is the welcome warmer or the standard of hospitality higher.

Reflecting on the fulfillment of his dream, Ernie Blake says, "We started this place for our own pleasure, and we've kept things simple. We've never operated beyond our means, nor have we allowed our guests to feel exploited. All we've ever wanted here are people who take skiing seriously, who love powder and who relish a personal and caring ski atmosphere in the true, old-fashioned European sense."

Inevitably and reluctantly, one asks what Taos will be like after Ernie is gone, a prospect as difficult to visualize as New Year's Eve once seemed without Guy Lombardo. Will there be high-rise condos on a precious parcel of what little undeveloped land remains in the valley? Will the parking lot be paved? Will there be more easy terrain? Will there be high-speed lifts? Will there even be foam pads on the chairs?

Some of these changes might come, but the extreme ones never will. As Chris Stagg put it, "Taos may change a little. But it will always be in a way that honors Ernie."

Amen.

Telluride, Colorado

NO ONE JUST STOPS BY
TELLURIDE. THE BOTTOM LINE
IS THAT PEOPLE GO THERE
BECAUSE THEY *REALLY* WANT TO

Telluride is what Aspen was like twenty years ago." That refrain is used by Telluride locals to explain their fondness for a used-up mining town in the middle of nowhere. They use it as an apology when the local airport is closed (again!) or when the unpaved side streets melt into quagmires at the height of spring skiing. They use it defiantly to imply that Telluride will never be permitted to become as chic and trendy as Aspen is today.

Literally and figuratively, Telluride is the end of the road. The main drag rises from the outskirts of town and dead-ends against the 14,000-foot peaks of the San Juan range. It is sixty-seven miles from Montrose, where Telluride-bound flights are regularly diverted, and half of that mileage is on narrow roads etched into mountainsides or flirting with streams in deep gorges. Telluride is also the end of the line for philosophical drop-outs and emigrés from ski towns that grew too big or too glamorous. It's a place where the counterculture still exists. In 1987, a white Rastafarian ran for Town Council, his strawberry blond dreadlocks jiggling as he campaigned along Colorado Avenue—and no one thought it weird.

Telluride is situated in a particularly rugged and beautiful area of the Rockies.

No one just stops by Telluride. The bottom line is that people go there because they *really* want to. Skiers in ever increasing numbers want to because of the three hundred inches of seamless powder laid on awesome ski terrain each winter. Because of its remoteness, liftlines are non-existent, and fresh powder remains fresh for days.

SKIING

Telluride has as wide and gentle a beginner meadow as any ski area in the world. Its intermediate runs in Gorrono Basin provide joyful ego-skiing on more than a dozen immaculately groomed runs. But the real reason to ski Telluride is for the mind-bending, knee-knocking steeps of the Front Face.

The Face looms right over town, all seriousness and challenge. Two chairlifts take off where the sidewalks stop. The Coonskin lift, designated Chair Seven, climbs to a saddle which accesses the delights of Gorrono. The Oak Street lift, Chair Eight, leads to Chair Nine, which unloads at

Telluride seeks to maintain
its historic western style.

Telluride's 11,890-foot summit. The view in every direction is more Alps than Rockies—a splendid panorama of sharp white peaks thrusting above the gentler dark green timberline. The view straight down is of a half dozen what-the-hell-am-I-doing-here-anyway? steeps that give Telluride its reputation as a true skier's mountain.

What you do is either bail out on See Forever, the long ridge run back to Gorrono, or you take a deep breath and go for it. You go for 3,155 vertical feet of precipitous, bump-studded trails like Kant-Mak-M, Mammoth, Spiral Stairs, or Plunge, respected for their relentless pitch and monster moguls.

Or you can ski Power Line, which in fact was the town's first source of electric power. Telluride was the first town in the United States with alternating current. The Gold King Mine had its own waterfall-driven hydroelectric generator and ran a line over the mountains to share this efficient new form of energy with the town. By the fifties, electricity came in from other sources, and local youngsters, bored with short rope tows, would hike up the mountain to ski the routes cut for poles and wires. Unmarked on Telluride's trail map, Power Line is wedged between Spiral Stairs and Plunge. It's thirty-five feet wide at best, and its grade is unforgiving.

When you've fried your thighs on the Front Face and think there are no blacker diamonds to be found, someone might suggest the double-black chutes up on Gold Hill. The wise skier begs off—or at least stops for a pizza and a beer at the Plunge Restaurant. It's been called the mountain oasis with the best view in the West, and the mountain company intends to expand it into a terrace restaurant cantilevered out over the valley. This small boxy place with big picture windows, however, hasn't yet grown into its name.

Having carbo-loaded on pizza and made courageous by alcohol at nearly 12,000 feet, you hike another 250 feet uphill to ski the Gold Hill Chutes, like Killer, Dynamo, and Electra. Compared to these powder chutes, which offer extreme skiing by anyone's standards, the expert runs below— off Chair Six, like Silver Glade and Apex—seem tame. In reality, Chair Six serves demanding high-altitude headwalls that would earn their diamonds on any mountain.

The lion's share of the presently developed acreage nestles in the sheltered precincts of Gorrono Basin. Here Telluride is not a mountain of fearsome steeps in the manner of Ajax or Alta, but a comfortable area for the casual tourist. Three chairlifts serve an appealing web of groomed trails, ranging from easy-does-it boulevards to intermediate trails of decent pitch. Sheltered in a mid-mountain hollow is Gorrono Ranch, a rustic-style complex that consists of a cafeteria, bar, ski school office, and spacious sun terrace.

Below, on the other side of the mountain *massif* from old Telluride, Telluride Mountain Village is in the first stages of development. Though it is presently just a huddle of condominiums, a sign announces it will be the site of the Franz Klammer Lodge, honoring the greatest downhill racer of modern times.

Below the Mountain Village is The Meadows, an astonishing beginner slope. Wide as a football field, this gentle practice slope is suited equally for shaky grownups and courageous small fry. Shooting off onto another peak is the Sunshine Express, at two miles the world's longest detachable quad chair. It presently accesses just two long low-intermediate trails, but it is the gateway for the planned expansion into Prospect Bowl. This will change Telluride's terrain from mostly advanced and expert to largely intermediate.

When undertaken, presumably in the early to mid-1990s if all necessary approvals are received, this expansion area, cupped in the vast cirque below Palmyra Peak, would include at least three more lifts and would triple the skiable acreage. Quantity isn't the only impressive thing about this ambitious plan; quality is the key, for it is to include European-style above-the-timberline bowl skiing within the reach of the average recreational skier.

Not unexpectedly, there developed a degree of clamor over Klammer and mayhem over the Mountain Village from the denizens of old Telluride. Even the most stereotypical anti-establishment types acknowledge that without tourists, there would be no jobs in shops and restaurants and lodgings. Neither they nor the entrepreneurs who've hired them want to see the center of skier activity move from the town to the new development, which is distant by road. So another project, which could come on line in the early 1990s, is a transit gondola, climbing over the hump between the Front Face and Gorrono Basin, a projected thirteen-minute ride in each direction.

In short, the town wants it both ways. It would like enough skiers to create a reasonably healthy economy, yet it doesn't want to be an urbanized resort with traffic jams, liftlines, and T-shirt shops on every corner. It pretends not to be impressed that Susan Saint James and Ralph Lauren have built designer homes on Wilson Mesa, but it does hope the celebrity dribble won't turn into a deluge. Whether the Mountain Village ever grows beyond a dream, whether or not there are three lifts or none in Palmyra Bowl, whether or not the transport gondola ever exists, high gloss is unlikely ever to come to Telluride. For skiers who come for the steep and deep are entranced with the ambiance of a place where the old lockup is now the public library, a former bordello has been turned into municipal offices, and the town hall was once Telluride's first school.

HISTORY

Telluride started as a mining camp when a prospector named John Fallon hit pay dirt in 1875, staking a mining claim that ultimately yielded $300 million of gold, silver, and tellurium, a metallic element used as an alloy in ceramics. It was a decade before the tents and shanties began to be replaced by real buildings. Eventually, solid brick structures of two and three stories lined Colorado Avenue, a boulevard so wide that a wagon pulled by a six-ox team could make a U-turn. It is now the core of the Telluride National Historic District, so designated in 1964.

Above Colorado Avenue, away from the ski mountain, was the refined neighborhood, where respectable families of mine owners lived in substantial gingerbread frame homes. Rowdy miners crammed into simple boarding houses below Colorado, and what they didn't sock away in the banks, drink away in the saloons, or gamble away in the sporting houses they spent in the "female boarding houses," mostly on Pacific Avenue where 175 girls were employed. Dance-hall girls like Silver Heels, gifted gamblers like Poker Alice, and madams like Diamond Tooth Leona provided all manner of diversion.

Along the avenue prosperity reigned. Elaborate saloons, well-provisioned stores, two newspaper offices, and a slew of banks were eloquent testimonials to Telluride's wealth. In 1889, Butch Cassidy made the first withdrawal of his infamous career from the San Miguel Valley Bank.

The New Sheridan Hotel was built in 1895, and from a scaffold erected outside the suite which now bears his name, William Jennings Bryan gave his famous Cross of Gold speech in 1903. Eleven years later, the New Sheridan Opera House was added to the hotel, serving as a grand ballroom in which dances, prizefights, and vaudeville shows took place. Lillian Russell, Sarah Bernhardt, and other stellar performers played at the Opera House. The lush nudes in the murals of the New Sheridan Bar now listen to the tales of bravado and bump skiing spun by legions of après-skiers, much as they overheard tall tales at the turn of the century.

RESTAURANTS

Telluride has the rough-edged look of a steak-and-potatoes town, but looks can be deceiving. Behind many saloon entrances are ambitious, thriving restaurants. Julian's, the handsome dining room in the New Sheridan Hotel, specializes in Italian regional cuisine, and *Gourmet* magazine published its recipe for lamb chops in Marsala sauce. But the restaurant that most enchanted the reporter from *Gourmet* was the Silverglade, which works magic in California style with pasta and seafood. Reservations are hard to obtain in this simply decorated downstairs eatery. La Marmotte serves outstanding French cuisine, and the New Powderhouse has a winning way with steak and seafood. La Gourmet Vite's food is just as good, but it's a takeout place favored by discriminating condo-dwellers.

Telluride isn't all gourmet surprises. There's casual eating at a slew of Colorado Avenue storefronts, like Sofio's for Mexican, Baked in Telluride for ethnic munchies ranging from bagels to *spanakopita*, the Excelsior and the Floradora for terrific breakfasts and casual lunches and dinners. Colorado Avenue is also the après-ski strip for informal, lively activities leaning toward western ambiance, a bit of rowdiness, and a lot of noise. There's music and maybe dancing or darts and pool at Cassidy's, O'Willy's, Fly Me to the Moon Saloon, the Roma Bar, and the Last Dollar.

LODGING

With the exception of the Bryan Suite, all the New Sheridan's rooms are spartan, as are the accommodations in a couple of bargain bed-and-breakfast places. There's also a handful of motels, but condominiums predominate. Most are within walking distance of the lifts, generously sized, and equipped with Jacuzzis. Condo complexes of no particular distinction have elaborately tiled whirlpools for a dozen sybarites, cozy redwood hot tubs ringed by Plexiglas walls to protect the whirlees from Colorado mountain breezes, or private outdoor Jacuzzis with matchless mountain views.

After all, the locals are right. Telluride is what Aspen was like twenty years ago: remote, funky, and great skiing.

Vail & Beaver Creek, Colorado

NO PLACE ELSE IN SKIDOM
HAS IT ALL — IN THE
DEPTH AND BREADTH OF VAIL

What Palm Beach is to sun worshipers and Pebble Beach is to golfers, Vail is to skiers. It is complete, compelling, and complex. There are other places with quaint town centers, lavish accommodations, fabulous shops . . . places with fine dining and splendid après-ski . . . places with exceptional travel convenience . . . places drawing the rich and famous . . . places with vast and varied ski terrain. But no place else in skidom has it all—in the depth and breadth of Vail.

As a resort, Vail is everyone's dream vacation. As a ski mountain, it is America's largest—with more acreage, more uphill capacity, and more annual skier visits than any other. Vail is spoken in the same breath as with the world's smartest ski resorts: Aspen, Courchevel, Kitzbühel, St. Moritz, Sun Valley, and Zermatt. And as if that weren't enough, it is paired with Beaver Creek, a new and very upscale development, ten miles away. Thirty years ago, Gore Creek Valley, parallel to U.S. Highway 6, was a bucolic vista of woods and sheep meadows. Today, Interstate 70 has replaced Route 6 as the main east-west highway through Colorado, and the view is of a multi-mile man-

The nightlife at Vail covers the spectrum, from haute cuisine to fireworks.

made skyline. In so short a time, Vail has developed into a real town, with housing for tens of thousands of residents and guests, two distinct downtown cores, schools, and even rush-hour traffic jams. The catalyst for this explosive growth is a huge *massif* that has been turned, quite simply, into the best over-all ski area in America. Its natural contours are made for skiing—a big lushly treed mountain that is hospitable rather than intimidating. What is visible from below is but a fraction of what Vail offers, for enfolded within its vast acreage are endless miles of ego-building skiing, gentle meadows for the most fragile beginners, steep-rimmed cirques that sprout nasty bumps, and the biggest lift-served bowl skiing in America.

While the personality of other ski mountains can be summed up with relative ease, Vail's is a combination of the best of them. It is the ideal learning hill, with wide gentle slopes blanketed with forgiving Colorado snow under the aegis of the country's largest ski school, a blue-jacketed army of some of the most effortlessly cheerful, best trained, and most competent instructors in the land. It is the consummate example of what intermediate skiers seek: long, carefully groomed trails that inspire new levels of speed, skill, and confidence. It is an exemplary expert's mountain, with demanding bump runs and bowls so vast that they bring the essence of the out-of-bounds experience safely within the area boundary.

SKIING

Vail Mountain is the country's largest single-mountain ski complex with thirteen square miles of ski terrain comprised of eighty-nine slopes and trails and more than seven hundred acres of lift-served powder bowls. It is Colorado's lift leader, both in terms of sheer numbers (one six-passenger gondola and nineteen chairlifts with an uphill capacity of over 35,000 passengers an hour) and in technology (six high-speed super-quads, the most anywhere). And it is one of a handful of U.S. ski areas whose vertical is over 3,000 feet. What is loosely called Vail encompasses not only the original ersatz-Alpine Vail Village, but also high-rise LionsHead; fashionable East Vail, where many locals live; West Vail, where so-called "budget" lodging can be found; Beaver Creek, ten miles to the west; Avon, a sprouting town at "the Beave's" base; Eagle-Vail between them; and Minturn, a once-decaying town up a side road toward Tennessee Pass. Even Edwards, a couple of miles west of Avon, now considers itself part of the complex. Vail Valley has become the Los Angeles of the ski world, and some long-time residents have still not seen it all or skied it all.

The original ski area that spawned this twenty-mile sprawl opened on December 15, 1962, with just a handful of buildings—a dream brought to life by Pete Seibert, who trained during the war with the Tenth Mountain Division at nearby Camp Hale. It started big and was designed to get bigger. Launched with one four-passenger gondola, two double chairlifts, and a beginner Pomalift, Vail was born as America's third-largest ski area. It debuted with the 3,150-foot vertical that is

Vail Village is a shopper's paradise.

skied to this day. The gondola, the country's first, lurched from the edge of what would grow into Vail Village to Mid-Vail, where muscular men manually braked each car as it slid into the top terminal. Below, long trails had been carved out of the fir and pine. From the Mid-Vail plateau, one chair climbed to the *massif's* summit, accessing six square miles of magnificent Back Bowls. Another chairlift ferried skiers out of the bowls back to the mountaintop. Vail was an instant success, the fifth-busiest ski area in the country by the end of its first winter, and the area has grown quickly and consistently.

Golden Peak, to the east, was developed as a teaching hill in 1967, and two years later, the

Making first tracks in the fabulous Back Bowls.

ski area was extended westward to LionsHead with a second gondola, a base-to-summit six-passenger lift. Vail Village continued expanding in its Alpine style, while a contemporary development grew at LionsHead.

In the 1985-86 season, Vail was purchased by a puckish Nashville millionaire named George Gillett, a long-time recreational skier before he bought into the business. His first move was to put in four high-speed quad lifts at once, at a cost of $10 million. It has been a masterstroke, unclogging Vail's legendary liftlines and grabbing publicity that would have done P.T. Barnum proud. One of the conventional quad express lifts, seating four abreast, goes up from Mid-Vail to serve novice and intermediate runs; another is in Game Creek Bowl for intermediate and advanced terrain; and a third is on Northwoods to service mogully Northeast Bowl. The fourth, which makes the run from Vail Village to Mid-Vail in nine minutes, is a Plexiglas-domed chair called the Vista Bahn.

The quads did everything they were supposed to. Lift lines have been slashed, uphill rides are quicker, and people have begun to ski the lower mountain for more than just the end-of-the-day run. They are lunching in the village because the ride back up is so short. People get in so much skiing with so little down-time to rest that they often queue up for lunch at eleven and voluntarily quit for the day at two. The ski area has had to expand its on-mountain eating facilities, and downtown businesses are geared up for early shoppers and après-skiers.

The only slopes that seem crowded are the intermediate runs on LionsHead and at Mid-Vail. Skiers are effectively dispersed all over the mountain, from gentle roads like Gitalong Road and Lion's Way to double-black pumpers like Highline and Blue Ox. They may stack up at a few of the chairs, especially the triple which hauls skiers out of the Back Bowls, but otherwise, Vail admirably handles the mobs.

Those bowls, scooped out of the back side of Vail Mountain, are a magnet unto themselves. One is called Sun Up, the other Sun Down, and the swale which divides them is High Noon Ridge. Legend has it that the indigenous Ute Indians, incensed at the white man's intrusion into their hunting lands in the 1800s, set spite fires which deforested the bowls. In fact, it was the discovery of these bowls by Pete Seibert and his sidekick Earl Eaton, when they were scouting the Gore Range more than thirty years ago, that inspired the development of Vail. There's plenty of room in the bowls for additional lifts, but to keep the feeling close to what Seibert and Eaton found, there is just one.

The Back Bowls' six square miles can hold a lot of people. After a night of snow, scores of skiers are ready when the lifts start running. They stand on the mountaintop, salivating for the rope drop that will open up oceans of white just waiting for tracks. The horde fans out, as each skier heads for his best-loved routes. Regular Vail skiers all have their favorites: the daunting pitches of Milt's Face or Headwall, the ricochet ride of seesawing from one bank to the other of The

Slot or Yonder Gulley, or powder dancing on Forever and Wow, which start as glades before opening up into tree-free steeps. Insiders have discovered super-secret places where the powder lasts longer and the challenge is magnified. The bad news is that these powder pigs go about their business so ferociously, so methodically, so relentlessly that the bowls can be skied out by noon. The good news is that the bowls are as wonderful clad in corn as in powder, and spring starts early in the bowls, thanks to their southern exposure.

Vail's new frontier is China Bowl, a prodigious powder paradise, which was accessible for snowcat skiing for three years before the installation of yet another super quad in 1988. Five new bowls—China, plus Tea Cup, Siberia, Mongolia (the last accessed by a new surface lift), and the expansion of the Sun Up Bowl—nearly doubles Vail's skiable acreage to 3,787 and stretches its terrain seven miles between the Cascade and Mongolia lifts. Envisioning its size is like trying to create a mental picture of Alaska. Skiing it can become a lifetime mission.

LODGING

Vail is not just a great ski resort. It is a posh and elegant vacation resort. For the affluent, Vail is chic, expensive, and exciting. But it is also a resort that the budget-conscious can enjoy—eschewing the Lodge at Vail for a condo on the north side of I-70 and chowing down at Pizza Hut instead of dining at Ambrosia. Skiing costs the same for all, and window shopping along Bridge Street is free.

Vail has more places to stay, play, and eat than any other ski resort. There are beds for 25,000 guests and tables in at least seventy restaurants, ranging from good to exceptional. In keeping with the Alpine ambiance of Vail Village, two of the most delightful establishments could be transplants from the heart of Europe. Gasthof Gramshammer, owned by ex-Austrian ski star Pepi Gramshammer, and his comely wife Sheika, is located centrally, and it has an excellent restaurant. Nearby is the equally atmospheric Sonnenalp, namesake of an outstanding Bavarian hotel.

Other top accommodations are larger and more American. The Lodge at Vail is a posh condo-hotel just steps from the Vista Bahn, while Manor Vail is similar, near Golden Peak. The Vail Athletic Club is an elegant, modern hotel on the outskirts of the village. The Westin at Vail, even sleeker, offers first-rate service and unparalleled convenience, for it now has its own lift to the LionsHead slopes. The LionsHead luxury leader is Marriott's Mark, an urban-looking, full-service hotel. The Vail Athletic Club and the Westin have huge, excellent, fully staffed health clubs—as does the Vail Racquet Club, whose main drawback is a distant location in East Vail.

RESTAURANTS

All of these upscale hotels also take pride in their first-rate restaurants. Manor Vail's Lord Gore, named after the English nobleman who first explored what is now Vail Valley, is a spacious restaurant specializing in beef, seafood, and game. Maison Creole in the Vail Athletic Club features New Orleans specialties. Alfredo's is a subdued, elegant northern Italian eatery in the Westin, while Windows atop the Marriott dishes up commendable Continental fare and a fabulous view. Other excellent restaurants include the Lancelot for prime rib, La Tour and the Left Bank for the finest French cuisine, and Sweet Basil for nouvelle American fare. Two Vail classics, the Ore House and the Red Lion—the latter as old as Vail itself—are tops for terrific steaks. It's possible to find everything from Mexican to Moroccan food, and visitors could dine out for weeks without retracing their tracks.

APRÈS-SKI

Vail's après-ski scene starts when skiers—weary, ebullient, or both—descend from the mountain to join the wouldn't-be-caught-skiing shoppers, wanderers, and party types who appear in the late afternoon. They mingle as they search for a perch where the mood fits. Right after the lifts close, Alfie Packer's packs 'em in, the Clock Tower Inn starts ticking, Pepi's perks, they're making killer margaritas at Matt's, and Frasier's is frenetic. More sedate sites for liquid sedation are the elegant lobby bars at the Vail Athletic Club and the Westin. After dinner, there's rock-n-roll music at Cyrano's, loud bands at the Red Lion, top-name entertainers at The Studio, and late-night mingling at the Hong Kong Cafe. The best dance spots are the Altitude Club, Bridge Street Cafe, and Cyrano's.

BEAVER CREEK

Even with all its skiing, dining, après-skiing, shopping, and mind-bending selection of non-ski activities from ice skating to rock aerobics, from tennis to snowmobile rentals, Vail is only one part of the experience. The other is Beaver Creek, one of the two most luxurious ski resorts ever built (The other is Deer Valley) and by far the larger. When Denver was planning to host the 1976 Winter Olympics, the Alpine ski events were slated for Vail, so Vail Associates bought a ranch above Avon and began mapping out a separate ski mountain where races could be held. Then Coloradans voted not to host the Games; the Olympics returned to Innsbruck, Austria, where they had been held in 1964; and Vail had a few more years to think about how Beaver Creek would take shape.

SKIING

They thought well, for the mountain—all 3,340 vertical feet of it—incorporates the best elements of ski area design. It's skiing for the executive suite and the BMW set: attractive, functional, ego-gratifying. Trails swoop along with the contours of the land, wide white rivers of snow dotted with islands of trees to add skiing interest and eye appeal.

Beaver Creek's main mountain has an abundance of cruising terrain. It's a mountain where some of the easier runs are way on top, enabling even low intermediates to appreciate the grand views. Solid medium runs compose the mid section, while slightly steeper terrain, groomed just as perfectly, is on the bottom. Access is via three consecutive chairlifts, including a high-speed quad, so skiers may run top to bottom or stay in the sector they prefer. The one continuous trail that does it all is Centennial. This run, first intended as the 1976 Olympic men's downhill venue, will fill that role during the 1989 World Alpine Championships. The great Swiss racer Bernhard Russi recontoured Lower Centennial with a 450-foot-long, 30-foot-deep trench that will add a thrilling bobrun-type element to what is already skiing's most exciting specialty.

There is pull-out-all-the-stops open-slope skiing on Larkspur Bowl and, to the constant astonishment of ultra-experts who denigrate the Beave as being too easy, a trio of double-diamond bump runs known as the Birds of Prey. The moguls on Golden Eagle, Goshawk, and Peregrine are as big as snow-covered Volkswagens.

Yet with all the excellent skiing at Beaver Creek, it is still nowhere near its capacity. Even on weekends, the lines are relatively short, largely because Front Range skiers won't add another ten miles to their drive, and vacationers who have chosen Vail tend to want to ski there—and only there.

LODGING, RESTAURANTS, AND APRÈS-SKI

Beaver Creek ambiance is epitomized by Beano's Cabin, reminiscent of the Adirondack Mountain "camps" of nineteenth-century New York millionaires. Hidden in a hollow near the base of Larkspur Bowl, Beano's is a huge log structure decorated with hunting trophies and set up as a private luncheon club. Members, mostly Beaver Creek homeowners, pay a hefty fee to lunch there on exquisite food, meticulously prepared and served, and privately billed.

Beaver Creek Village is small, yet dramatic, with massive buildings of pastel stucco, stone, wood, lightened with arches and gables, balconies and tiled roofs, towers and bays. The effect is at once powerful, whimsical, and elegant—and, above all, expensive. Village Hall serves as a base lodge, commercial center, and general activities hub. Nearby are fabulous accommodations, located on or near the slopes, beautifully furnished. A suite at the Charter Lodge, Park Plaza Lodge, Poste Montane, or any other Beaver Creek property is synonymous with the highest standard of luxury. Flanking the traffic-restricted access road (Buses shuttle day skiers from the parking lot near Avon) and the lower ski runs are multi-million-dollar vacation homes. The Gerald Fords, long-time Vail skiers, selected Beaver Creek for their new vacation home. From Chair 12, it is possible to look right down on the Ford house, distinguished from its neighbors by the small guardhouses where Secret Service agents are posted when the former First Couple is in residence.

Evenings are quieter at Beaver Creek than at Vail. There is no opportunity to promenade as in Vail Village and LionsHead. Après-ski is more likely to be cocktails in the condo than beer at the base. The Legends in the Poste Montane and Drinkwater Park or McCoy's in Village Hall are the liveliest spots. The Charter has a piano bar. The best dining is at Mirabelle's, an old ranch house that is now an exquisite French restaurant. The Four Seasons in the Charter is known for game. The Legends (American dishes) and Drinkwater's (Mexican) have more moderately priced offerings. And at night, Beano's accommodates the hoi polloi who may book a dinner sleighride.

Vail will be the site of the 1989 World Alpine Championships, the first time this ultra-prestigious biennial has been held in the United States since Aspen hosted it in 1950. The downhill will be run on Beaver Creek's Centennial, and the other events will be on Vail Mountain. The bets are that it will be the best-organized world championship ever. For "best" is the only way Vail does anything.

Winter Park, Colorado

WITH BLOOMINGDALE FACILITIES AT
K-MART RATES, WINTER PARK IS
REGULARLY SELECTED AS
"COLORADO'S FAVORITE SKI RESORT"

Winter Park has been called the best-kept secret in skidom. It is one of the oldest ski areas in the Rockies, yet it is one of the newest vacation resorts. Owned by the City of Denver and located just sixty-seven miles away, it started as a day-trip area, then blossomed into a weekend area, and more recently became a destination resort too. While it remains a weekend playground for locals, more than half its skiers are now vacationers. Accommodations span the spectrum from old-fashioned lodges to fancy condos, all at prices below the Colorado norm. Winter Park, now spread over three interconnected peaks with a promise of more, is all things to all skiers. There is terrain for skiers of all ability levels. It is a mellow place, especially suitable for families.

Few places have contributed so much to skiing over so many years. Skiers began showing up in the late twenties, climbing up and skiing down a hill just outside the Moffat Tunnel, the six-mile railroad tunnel under the Continental Divide. In 1934, this sunny tract was purchased for the City of Denver by Parks Superintendent George Cranmer. A small railroad station at the base of the slopes made this a most accessible mountain, and hordes of happy Denverites commuted

Amtrack provides daily service to Winter Park from Denver.

via ski train to ride the single rope tow and ski a half-mile-long slope.

En route to the big leagues, Winter Park pioneered grooming, base-lodge design, and skiing for the handicapped. The first two brainstorms came from the fertile mind of Steve Bradley, a one-time Dartmouth ski racer who piloted the area through the fifties and sixties. The Bradley Packer, a drum rolling behind a fast-skiing patrolman much the way a rescue toboggan is towed, was the first practical grooming device. And the spacious Balcony House, the first base facility that was more than a warming hut, was designed on passive solar principles back in 1955. (Also in the fifties, Comet and Meteor were the world's fastest T-bars, a legacy now honored with new high-speed chairlifts.)

The third breakthrough, skiing for the disabled, was developed by instructor Hal O'Leary. His award-winning teaching techniques and ski equipment modifications have made it possible for amputees, cerebral palsy sufferers, Down's syndrome children, and others with physical or developmental handicaps to ski. At Winter Park, the world's largest center for teaching the disabled to ski, amputees with outriggers instead of ski poles, parapelegics in kayak-like sleds, and blind skiers trailed by seeing-eye skiers share the slopes with "normies," as those who are handicapped call those who are not.

The Sun Valley Lodge and Baldy as seen from one of the Lodge's hot pools.

Cliff Robertson, Mary Hart, Marjoe Gortner, Brooke Shields, Ed Begley, Jr., and George Hamilton celebrate Sun Valley's fiftieth anniversary.

The view of Seattle Ridge from the deck of Lookout.

Extensive nighttime grooming makes for excellent daytime cruising.

Ernie Blake found his ideal ski mountain in the Sangre de Cristo Range.

Steep and deep during a heavy snow.

Après-ski on a sunny deck.

TELLURIDE, COLORADO

Behind the western facade are good restaurants and great hot tubs.

No liftlines and long-lasting powder are among the attractions.

Many skiers feel that the town of Telluride is the way that Aspen used to be.

There are beautiful uncrowded cruising runs at Beaver Creek.

VAIL & BEAVER CREEK, COLORADO

Beaver Creek's luxury resort village.

World Cup racing.

Jean Claude Killy, Jimmie Heuga, and Billy Kidd.

Vail Valley, a twenty-mile sprawl of development, offers some of the biggest and best skiing in America.

Events like the Spring Splash help make
Winter Park Colorado's favorite ski resort.

Winter Park's facilities make it particularly suitable for families.

The ski school conducts bump skiing workshops.

Sugarbush has skiing for all levels plus activities for kids.

Mont St. Anne is a modern ski mountain just thirty minutes from Quebec City.

The historic western town of Crested Butte, Colorado, is located only two miles from the ski area.

There's skiing from November to July at Mount Bachelor, Oregon.

More than five hundred inches of powder falls at Grand Targhee.

The luxurious Chet Huntley Lodge at Big Sky, Montana.

Clear blue skies and fresh powder are a heli-skier's dream.

The Bugaboo Lodge is one of the remote outposts of CMH Heli-skiing.

Heli-skiing can be an adventure of a lifetime.

The tiny resort of Sunshine Village offers bowl skiing and over four hundred inches of powder annually.

The Banff Springs Hotel is a summer resort hotel that becomes a ski lodge in winter.

Lake Louise is the biggest ski area in the Canadian Rockies.

The Whistler/Blackcomb area offers world class skiing just seventy miles from Vancouver.

Whistler Village has excellent hotels and is the most convenient place to stay.

Whistler offers a wide variety of different runs.

Winter Park is big,
easy to reach, and reasonably priced.

For years, Winter Park was known as the place folks from the Mile High City learned to ski. But Winter Park's growth over five decades has been inextricably linked to transportation and the accessibility of newer areas. As ski trains gave way to cars, Winter Park was still a prime choice. U.S. Route 6, the major east-west highway and gateway to the Rockies was so scary, with harrowing hairpin turns as it crossed the Continental Divide at Loveland Pass, that many skiers preferred U.S. 40 over Berthoud Pass near Winter Park. New skiers started driving the easier pass and learning to ski on the easier mountain.

This pattern changed when the Eisenhower Tunnel was drilled under the Divide in the late sixties, giving easy access to the new Summit County areas and even to more remote Vail. Berthoud Pass began looking hairier. Congenial as Winter Park remained, Denver skiers seemed ready to turn in their comfortable old shoes for fancy slippers to dance on other mountains. It looked for a brief, bleak moment as if Denver might jilt Winter Park.

But area management quickly reacted. In 1975, Mary Jane, a separate, spectacular mountain was opened. Sustained fall-line skiing and banzai bumps make the Jane a tough mistress even for the local macho hotshots who court her each weekend. In 1986-87, when Aspen, Keystone, and Steamboat stole the promotional thunder with their new high-tech gondolas, Winter Park had the greatest terrain expansion in the Centennial State—thirty-three new trails and a total of three hundred additional acres—but got a lot less publicity for its investment.

Nevertheless, savvy Denver skiers, always alert to what's newest and best, embraced the expansion area as they have everything Winter Park has ever done. Marketing surveys regularly show it to be "Colorado's favorite ski resort." Its appeal for locals is not lost on vacationers either. Blissfully uncrowded during the week, it is convenient and reasonably priced—Bloomingdale's facilities at K-Mart rates.

SKIING

There are ski areas with far greater vertical drops—Winter Park's is a modest 2,200 feet—but it takes a backseat to none in terms of other measurements. Three peaks encompass over 915 skiable acres, the fifth-largest in the state. There are a dozen double chairlifts, three triples, and a trio of quads with an uphill capacity of 24,000 skiers an hour, right behind Vail and Steamboat.

The main base complex has the old Balcony House and West Portal Station, a spacious, modern facility with a sensational sun terrace. The skiing is etched onto a series of peaklets that push against the soaring summits of the Divide. The handful of runs visible from the bottom present only a preview of Winter Park's vastness, since the ski terrain scales a series of rises and plateaus that are not visible from the base.

Runs that have been favorites for generations of regulars include Bradley's Bash and Balch, two fall-line straight-shooters. Bradley's is usually groomed; Balch is usually bumps. Below them is Wilson's Way, a sheltered, fenced-off beginner slope served by a low, slow chair, used for teaching first-timers and people in the handicap program. Arching behind this peak are Cranmer and Alan Phipps, two perennial favorites of steady pitch and uncommon width. On another face are Engel Dive and Over 'n Underwood, two short ego-building black runs. All the trails on this sector are named after Winter Park pioneers or people instrumental in its growth.

Nestled in a hollow where this web of runs comes together is Snoasis, one of the earliest mid-mountain restaurants in the Rockies. The congenial and popular cafeteria overflows on weekends with hungry skiers who prefer not to return to West Portal Station. A shortcut to a full tummy is the pizza phone at Sunspot, the mountain's summit. People use it to place their orders and ski down to Snoasis where their pie will be waiting at Mama Mia's Pizzeria.

To the north of these main runs, over the next ridge, is Winter Park's newest terrain. Fairyland is a small network of easy runs named after Alice in Wonderland characters, and still farther is Vasquez Ridge, opened in 1986-87, and served by the Pioneer Express, a high-speed quad. It has a respectable 1,250 vertical, and, because it is on the fringes of the ski area, it never gets crowded. Original plans called for just four trails, but once the crews started cutting, the terrain was so good that they laid in first eight and finally thirteen intermediate and advanced trails. Vasquez' charms have only begun to unfold, for this will be the hub of another expansion phase. There is to be a town gondola from below and eventually expansion to Vasquez Mountain above.

Hunkering at the southern end of Winter Park is Mary Jane. It is like a ski area within a ski area, with separate base facilities and connected to the main mountain only via two upper trails and a lower catwalk. Its steady fall-line trails threaded through the dense woods look different and ski differently. Steady pitches and big bumps lure the strongest skiers. The Jane's own weather pattern means an average of ten feet more snow each season than the rest of Winter Park. Regular grooming is imposed on only a handful of trails, ones that are easy for Mary Jane but would range at the upper end of the spectrum on the Winter Park side.

The Mary Jane parking lot is the first one out from Denver, and many iron-legged regulars never even get to the main mountain—to say nothing of the town beyond. The ski school's bump-skiing workshops are given by a rough-and-ready corps of instructors who call themselves the Jane Gang. The Jane's meanest mogul runs sport the oddest names. Years back, before indoor plumbing, there was an outhouse on Sunspot. When people said they were going to the outhouse, they often were really sneaking off for some tree skiing where Mary Jane is, so now the access run into the Jane is called Outhouse. Drunken Frenchman was named for the French-Canadian logger who headed the trail crews. Many of the runs are narrow by Colorado standards and some have lovely islands of trees in their midst.

Mary Jane grew by 50 percent with the addition of Mary Jane's Backside, a broad-beamed web of gladed runs and narrow steeps that comprises the other part of the 1986-87 expansion. It will ultimately be a gateway to Parsenne Bowl, a mouthwatering cirque of high snowfalls, powder chutes, and sharp headwalls enfolding everything from the Backside to the Vasquez in one white embrace. Timetables are hard to get when ski companies must consider government permits, interest rates, and market demand, but the mid-nineties is not an unreasonable guess for Winter Park's buildout.

Back at West Portal Station is the two-story Children's Center, another facility that sets this resort apart. The center contains everything for youngsters under one roof: toddler nursery, junior rental shop, indoor play area for young skiers between lessons, staging area for older children who spend the day on the mountain, and even separate kitchens where time-tested kidfood is prepared. Right outside the door is Penguin Peak, a lilliputian hill where the youngest children have their ski lessons. Parents may hover on a secluded deck overlooking this fenced-off area, unseen from below, to watch their little ones ski. The Children's Center, which can accommodate up to seven hundred youngsters, is off-limits to anyone but participants, a secure arrangement bringing peace of mind to parents.

LODGING

What the resort has thus far lacked is an identifiable town center. Downtown was until recently a wide spot on Route 40 with a few motels, a couple of gas stations, a handful of ski shops, a post office, and a number of convenience stores. The void was partly remedied with the development of Cooper Creek Square, an attractive brick mall that will be the center of future development.

Most of the places to stay are tucked into the piney woods and served by an excellent, free shuttle bus system. There are few fancy hotels, but popular priced lodging abounds. Some are informal lodges, almost in the New England tradition, where the cozy rooms and sometimes two squares a day are still bargains. Most of the other accommodations are in condominiums. Brenner's Ski Chalet and Millers Inn are small lodges in the old style. The Sitzmark is a big old lodge on Route 40, while Woodspur sprawls on a hilltop. Hideaway Village are true economy condos, and Kings Crossing are solar townhouses surrounded by aspens.

The most elegant development is the Iron Horse. Attractive and contemporary, nestled between the Winter Park and Mary Jane bases, it is the only ski-in, ski-out facility. Well-appointed, it has a terrific outdoor pool, small health club, and a restaurant. Another leading complex is the Silverado II, with a topnotch fitness center in the valley, a restaurant, and spacious suites.

APRÈS-SKI AND RESTAURANTS

There's enough after-ski to last a week, although sorting the spots out can be confusing to outlanders. Did you say you were meeting at The Slope, The Shed, or The Stampede—or was it The Carousel or The Kitchen? The Slope, an expanded A-frame near the mountains, is a Winter Park after-ski tradition. Its appeals are a busy downstairs bar and a fine dining room. The Shed, a cozy place, also has a lively après-ski scene, plus steaks, burgers, and Mexican fare. The Stampede at Cooper Creek Square is a huge club with two bars, a big disco, and a restaurant with excellent breakfasts. The Carousel is a northern Italian restaurant, also in Cooper Creek Square, and The Kitchen is best known for good, Mexican-style breakfasts.

Deno's Swiss House is a lively sports bar with several TVs showing the game of the week, or the day, or the hour. In addition to pizza and bar food in the lounge, the casual Coachman Tavern does ribs, steaks, and Mexican specialties. Its former owners, Hannes and Hannelore Eichler, went on to create the award-winning Gasthof Eichler, known for excellent German and other continental fare. The Eichlers have built a new European-type bed-and-breakfast lodge, which adds another style of quality hostelry to the Winter Park scene.

Five miles to the north is Fraser, where many Winter Park employees live. A resort atmosphere, however, is slowly creeping up on Fraser. Condo developments are spreading along the hillsides above Route 40 between the two towns, and skiers are joining locals in bars and restaurants. The Crooked Creek Saloon has nightly live music and an array of specialties that range from the awesome Fat Boy Burger, a ten-ounce mound of meat accompanied by a ton of fixings, to Rocky Mountain Oysters, a delicacy rarely found even in the heart of the Rocky Mountains.

People go to Winter Park for the convenience and the skiing, not for non-stop nightlife or an infinite variety of restaurants. But with the convenience so great and the skiing so good, Colorado's favorite area has made it as a top resort too.

The Best of the Rest, East

LAKE PLACID/WHITEFACE MOUNTAIN, NEW YORK

Lake Placid, which isn't on Lake Placid but on Mirror Lake, used to be a lovely little town regarded as the winter-sports capital of America. Today, sadly in need of rehabilitation (and architectural and zoning standards compatible with its magnificent Adirondack surroundings), it is a homely little town which still lays claim to being the winter-sports capital of America, because it is the country's only two-time Winter Olympic site.

For its first Olympics, in 1932, the ice skating rink was built in an Art Deco arena, and the ski jumps and bobrun were constructed of wood—while the speedskating races were on the lake and Alpine skiing was not even on the program. For the second Olympics, in 1980, a new rink was built in a high-tech arena, a permanent refrigerated track was built for speedskating, new ski jumps and a combined, refrigerated luge/bobsled run were constructed of concrete—and Alpine ski races were held on the steep, rocky slopes of Whiteface Mountain. Lake Placid, now the official training center for Olympic hopefuls in all the winter sports, hosts a calendar full of competitions in all of them.

With 3,126 vertical feet, Whiteface is the highest ski mountain in the East—and one of the most demanding. Although trails were widened and snowmaking was added for (and since) the Olympics, the upper mountain remains a web of challenging, wind-swept runs. A twin-peak layout with separate chairs serving the upper mountain enables experts to stick to only the tough runs.

The lower slopes are easier, and there is an isolated novice area at the bottom. Whiteface is state-owned, so every improvement requires government approval—a predictable roadblock to steady, rapid enhancement of the facilities.

MONT SAINTE-ANNE, QUEBEC

Mont Sainte-Anne is unique in more ways than you can shake a ski pole at. With a distinctive Quebecois ambiance, it is the continent's most foreign, most flavorful, most French ski resort. A rare south-facing mountain on a 2,050-foot vertical, its front slopes catch whatever warming rays the midwinter sun may provide and also offer grand views of the St. Lawrence River. It is a thoroughly modern mountain, with two high-speed detachable quad chairs (one a Plexiglas-bubbled model) and a constantly upgraded snowmaking system. While the front face remains the most memorable, three dozen long runs, mostly intermediate and advanced, ripple down three mountain faces. Nearby is a world-class cross-country center with over one hundred miles of double-track trails.

The ski area benefits from its proximity (a half-hour's drive) to Quebec City, North America's only walled city, with a European atmosphere and the liveliest winter carnival north of New Orleans. For years, most skiers stayed in the city's four-star hotels, including the fabled Chateau Frontenac, and commuted to the mountain. Now a full resort is rapidly forming around one long-standing lodge and a scattering of condominiums at the base of Mont Sainte-Anne, making Quebec City an attractive side trip instead of a requirement for vacation pleasure.

MOUNT SNOW, VERMONT

As the closest major ski area to the New York metropolitan area, Mount Snow is a medium-size mountain that skis big. Anyone who has skied its long, fall-line runs feels as if more than 1,800 vertical feet have slipped beneath his skis. Most of the handsome front-of-the-mountain terrain was cut as wide, straight cruising runs long before that type of run had a name. The black-diamond trails on the North Face are as steep, narrow, and mogully as they come. Mount Snow, owned by Killington's parent company, has a different style from Killington but shows the same emphasis on reliable snow, monstrous uphill capacity, and a no-nonsense approach to providing popular packages and services. As a result Mount Snow has an ever-increasing census of lifts (sixteen, including a high-speed quad added in 1987 to replace an old gondola), trails (seventy-six, including eighteen annexed with the purchase of Carinthia in 1986), and excellent snowmaking (covering 80 percent of the terrain), and it offers attractive multi-day packages, excellent beginner programs, and a host of family-pleasing activities.

Skiers throng to southern Vermont, a region of gentle landscapes and lovely vistas. The younger groups bring lots of action to the Mount Snow après-ski scene, while the slightly older generation enjoys the traditional New England atmosphere at charming country inns and quiet gourmet restaurants.

Mount Snow in southern Vermont is a favorite resort for New Yorkers.

MOUNT WASHINGTON VALLEY, NEW HAMPSHIRE

The Attitash, Mount Cranmore, and Wildcat ski areas are scattered in the broad shadow of Mount Washington, the highest peak east of the Rockies. The main ski town is North Conway, known as a lively mecca for the young crowd, for factory outlet shopping, as well as for its historic role as the prime ski-train destination for Bostonians. The secondary ski town is Jackson, with even a stronger New England flavor.

Attitash is a mid-size family ski area with lots of good intermediate skiing, a reputation for excellent snowmaking and snow grooming, and a convenient across-the-street condo cluster. Mount Cranmore, celebrating its fiftieth anniversary in 1988, retains an air of old-fashioned skiing. Well located on the edge of downtown North Conway, the area is in the midst of some long-needed refinements. Known for its wide ski slopes and picturesque Skimobile, it has finally added modern lifts with decent uphill capacity, snowmaking, an expanded base lodge, and on-site lodging. Wildcat, atop Pinkham Notch, is the valley's biggest, most rugged ski area. Although it has two new triple chairlifts, increased snowmaking, and some trail widening, it still comes across as a tough mountain where advanced skiers find suitable challenge.

SKI BEECH/SUGAR MOUNTAIN, NORTH CAROLINA

With two of the South's three biggest ski resorts within four miles, Banner Elk, North Carolina, would be one of America's more important ski towns if it weren't nearly dry (only wine may be sold by the glass). The action, therefore, is at the resorts, which have taken Utah-style tacks around anti-liquor regulations. Both Beech and Sugar sprang from the fertile imagination of Tom Brigham, the skiing dentist credited with bringing the sport to Dixie. The two areas, under different ownership, are unfortunately not hooked up with a joint lift pass.

The resorts are as different as peanut butter and jelly. Beech, a squat, flat-topped mountain with a variety of runs spread across a broad face, installed the first high-speed detachable quad chair south of the Mason-Dixon Line. The resort development is distinctive for its quasi-Tyrolean look. Sugar, taller by 350 vertical feet, has a skinnier trail setup with narrow runs aimed straight down the fall line. Its resort development is of a contemporary design with natural wood predominating. The steep upper runs offer the most challenge, though the bottom is all run-out. Both Beech and Sugar have large ski schools, especially adept at turning legions of Southern drawlers, to whom snow is a foreign substance, into enthusiastic skiers who hoot and holler and love the white stuff.

SMUGGLERS' NOTCH, VERMONT

Smugglers' may not be one of Vermont's biggest ski areas, but it's a heavyweight in family skiing. A small village built of clapboard painted in traditional New England colors, but with strictly modern amenities, huddles at the base of Morse Mountain, a nice novice hill where beginners and small children ski comfortably. A ride up the Morse chair and a quick run down to a sheltered valley leads skiers to the main base area, with lifts rising in two directions to the tops of Sterling and Madonna Mountains. Sterling is largely intermediate, while Madonna boasts ultra-steep, ultra-narrow expert runs down the fall line under or near the longest chairlift. Because Smugglers' has only slow, old double chairs, liftlines may form. But the skiing experience itself is pleasurable because the slope space far outstrips lift capacity.

Smugglers' has made base development a priority, including the new Village Center, a multi-purpose lodge added in 1987-88, and the lush Aquacenter with indoor swimming, co-ed sauna, and great hot tubs. Family facilities and programs prevail, including an excellent nursery, a junior ski school, and evening activities for youngsters.

SNOWSHOE, WEST VIRGINIA

This remote ski area high in the Appalachian Mountains calls itself "the island in the sky." That's an appropriate slogan for this isolated spot of bright lights and white slopes in the midst of the rural highlands. Snowshoe, like Beech and Sugar, a creation of Dr. Tom Brigham, is the biggest ski area in the South. The resort perches atop a high ridge called Cheat Mountain with ski terrain dropping off both sides. The front runs range from a super-flat beginner slope next to the lodge to steep, mogully trails with tricky double fall lines. The Cupp Run on the other side is a mile of great, wide intermediate cruising—arguably the best run in mid-America. It alone has the area's advertised 1,500-foot vertical (twice that of the front face), and it is worth a trip through the tortuous country roads that pass for highways in West Virginia. The living is conve-

Snowshoe in West Virginia is the largest ski area in the South.

nient, the après-ski ranges from lively to downright rowdy, and Snowshoe remains the standout of southern skiing and ski life.

STRATTON, VERMONT

When a small child draws a ski mountain, it looks like a primitive rendition of Stratton: a conical peak, broad at the base, pointed at the top, and laced between with a dense network of trails. Eighty-six runs—fifty-one miles in all—are wrapped around three faces of the thickly wooded mountain. Wide, mild beginner and low-intermediate slopes in front of the Tyrolean-style base lodge are accessed by five lifts. Narrow high-intermediate and expert trails are served by a trio of upper chairlifts, two triples and a quad. And a twelve-passenger, stand-up gondola—the first in America— was added in 1988-89. Mid-level cruising slopes, including the extra-wide supertrail concept pioneered by Stratton, are on the right shoulder, and sheltered low-intermediate terrain is in the Sun Bowl on the mountain's southern side.

Long favored by skiing families from the wealthy suburbs around New York, Stratton is a place to find BMWs in the parking lots and Bogners on the slopes. Snowmaking, grooming, and the Austrian-accented ski school are excellent. Stratton has recently added a substantial slopeside development featuring condos, a new hotel (in addition to three existing ones), an excellent health spa, a lively village center, and a clock tower, obligatory for maintaining the Austro-Vermont ambiance which it has nurtured for a quarter of a century. Après-ski and shopping spill over to Manchester, as picture-postcard a Vermont town as ever there was. The Equinox, a historic landmark that was shuttered for years before being refurbished into an elegant inn, is the best place to stay in Manchester.

SUGARBUSH/MAD RIVER GLEN, VERMONT

Sugarbush is two mountains wedded under single ownership. Like any couple, they have much in common and much that is different. The original Sugarbush enjoyed a meteoric rise to glamour status in the early sixties when Stein Eriksen ran the ski school and assorted Kennedys cavorted there. It is still a choice area for eastern skiers willing to drive a little farther than mid-Vermont for a lot more mountain. The terrain divides into four sectors. The Village/Gate House runs are best for novices and newly minted intermediates. The Valley House section has a couple of blue cruisers but is best for its short, steep mogul trails. When the old three-place gondola served the network of black-diamond runs off the summit of the main mountain, people said they were "skiing the gondola." Now, the summit is reached by two triple chairs, Sugar Bravo and Heaven's Gate. The chairs enable them to choose just the upper runs, the lower ones, or both. The Castle Rock sector is high-expert with a half-dozen awesome mogul trails that make all of Sugarbush's other black diamonds pale into gray.

A short shuttle bus ride away is Mount Ellen at Sugarbush, originally called Glen Ellen and later Sugarbush North. The mountain is configured in wedding-cake tiers, with gentle terrain at the base, medium runs on mid-mountain, and steep, bumpy twisters off the North Ridge and Summit double chairs. Between Sugarbush and Mount Ellen is Slide Brook, a valley which, when outfitted with lifts as Sugarbush hopes to do sometime in the 1990s, will create one of America's biggest single ski areas.

Sharing the valley but not the Sugarbush lift ticket is Mad River Glen, an immutable classic of New England skiing. Steep trails, old lifts (including what must be the last single chair in captivity), and a disdain for any but the most elementary snowmaking and grooming characterize this demanding mountain. The trail map claims some beginner and intermediate terrain, but Mad River is mostly for experts—often three generations of loyalists who would ski nowhere tamer, nowhere milder, nowhere else.

Sugarbush Village was the first major slopeside development in Vermont, with easy-access condominiums and a health and sports spa that set the standard for others in New England. Elsewhere in the Warren-Waitsfield area are off-campus condos, lovely country inns, and a handful of traditional ski lodges, as well as lively après-ski spots and fine restaurants.

SUNDAY RIVER, MAINE

No ski area in Maine or New Hampshire (and few in the country) has developed with the speed and success of Sunday River. "Explosive" is the only adjective that adequately describes the growth of a ski area that went, in less than a decade, from a small hill with a handful of T-bars to a three-peak resort with fifty-six trails, a huge snowmaking plant, ten chairlifts (including three high-speed detachable quads), and one lone T-bar as a reminder of the way things were. The skiing is mostly novice through upper intermediate, on meticulously cared-for runs, though in 1988-89 it barreled into the experts' consciousness with the new White Heat run, billed as the steepest, longest, widest lift-served trail in the East. Sunday River is learn-to-ski heaven, offering—among other programs—a guarantee that a new skier will be able to navigate the bunny slope after just one day on skis.

The ski area is now also a full-fledged ski resort, with 3,500 beds in slopeside condos that are cozy and convenient. Sunday River is comfort more than luxury, reliability more than challenge—all people-pleasing considerations that have caused its skier visits to skyrocket by as much as 60 percent a year since the steady expansion and improvement program began.

The Best of the Rest, West

BIG SKY, MONTANA

Anyone who has skied Big Sky usually feels like a discoverer of skiing's last secret: a large mountain with small crowds. The scenery in this remote section of Montana, close to Yellowstone National Park, is simply stunning. The skiing on two mountains is exceptional for intermediates and improving for advanced skiers. Big Sky's big mountain is Lone Mountain, accessed by a pair of gondolas to two points part-way up the mountain. Gondolas, excellent choices for the bone-chilling days of the northern Rockies, open a neat network of runs that inspire medium skiers to soar. A high bowl, deeply sculpted under the mountain's Matterhorn-like summit, is the truly rare intermediate powder bowl. And a new double chair serves advanced terrain—former hike-in territory—on Little Rock Tongue and Big Rock Tongue. Andesite, the next mountain over from the main section, offers shorter intermediate runs on two faces.

Big Sky was founded by the late Chet Huntley, the newscaster and native Montanan, who had a dream of bringing major-league skiing to his state. Now owned by Boyne USA, the Michigan ski-area operator, it has a natural tie to the midwestern market. Because the resort is so remote that it can verge on the lonely, the conviviality of the luxurious Huntley Lodge is welcome. For those who prefer privacy, there are condos at and near the base. Big Sky also affords an opportunity for true western living at the Lone Mountain Ranch, a rustic resort built of log and stone in 1926.

BOGUS BASIN, IDAHO

If Bogus Basin were near Denver or Salt Lake City, its skiable acreage and frequent powder dumps would make it a knock-out destination. Because it is sixteen miles from Boise, it remains the biggest and one of the best day-trip mountains in America, and almost peripherally, the secret preserve of canny skiers from the Pacific Northwest who like the snow deep, the skiing casual, and prices low. Started in 1938 as a WPA project, the Basin still has such quirks as a hundred-bend access road. The trade-off for the drive is 2,000 acres of terrain, spread out on 1,800 vertical feet. Located on the western slope of the Rockies, the Basin claims the first effects of Pacific storms, yet with a summit elevation of just 7,590 feet, lower than the base of anything in Colorado, it's a good choice for skiers who don't do well at high altitude.

The skiing—about 80 percent for intermediate and advanced skiers—sprawls over ridges, down valleys, and across peaks. While over forty trails appear on the map, powder players skip through the trees, snowfields, and mogul fields frequently frosted with new snow. There is night skiing on about a third of the terrain. And skiing is basically what the area offers at night, for there is virtually no other nightlife to speak of.

CRESTED BUTTE, COLORADO

Crested Butte is one of North America's fastest-growing resorts. Just fourteen miles from Aspen as the proverbial crow flies, it is a drive measured in hours over you-can't-get-there-from-here mountain roads. Crested Butte's isolation was its salvation. The town, a delightful melange of cheerily re-done nineteenth-century buildings, was not compromised before it became a national historic district. The charm is downtown, enabling the mountain resort, two miles up the road, to develop with an emphasis on contemporary convenience rather than atmosphere.

Under the ownership of Howard "Bo" Calloway, a member of former President Jimmy Carter's Georgia Mafia, Crested Butte first began attracting southerners for whom low-level skiing and a friendly "howdie, y'all" atmosphere sufficed. The resort grew slowly with condos at the base, some lift and terrain expansion, and finally the addition of the deluxe Grande Butte Hotel. The extension of the airport at Gunnison, half an hour away, encouraged the resort to begin guaranteeing direct flights from major southern and midwestern airports.

The ski terrain wraps around a mountain that looks like a truncated Matterhorn. Most of the runs are either easy to middling—or very challenging. Mild pitches and wide, groomed swaths make the traditional Crested Butte vacationer happy, and the bump runs off the main chairlift fry the thighs of young hotshots. People also choose the Butte for an abundance of steep, out-of-bounds skiing. Hundreds of acres of hike-in terrain, patrolled but ungroomed, have been the private playground of locals known as some of the best powder skiers in Colorado. In 1987-88, Crested Butte took the unprecedented step of adding a short Pomalift to the tough terrain on the North Face. Lift access has eliminated the hike to the succession of waterfall steeps, cornices, and chutes comprising the terrain, now easier to get to but still not groomed and no easier to ski. The Butte is on its way to national renown.

GRAND TARGHEE, WYOMING

"Snow from heaven, not hoses" is a favorite slogan at Grand Targhee, a little jewel that claims more than five hundred inches of snow each winter. With a minuscule bed base and no near neighbors, it has so few skiers that liftlines are non-existent and the powder lasts and lasts. Targhee's unusual mailing address—Alta, Wyoming via Driggs, Idaho—is five words that speak volumes about its location. It pushes against the state line an hour west of Jackson Hole, drawing skiers on day trips from its larger, more famous Teton neighbor. The rest come because Grand Targhee is a grand bargain. Lift and lodging prices, enticingly low to begin with, are further enhanced by freebies for children under twelve on multi-day packages: free lodging, skiing, airport transfers, and, for some ages, instruction and rental equipment or nursery care. Families give up a lot of nightlife for that kind of deal.

The skiing is on a 2,200-foot vertical, nearly as high as Mount Mansfield at Stowe; 1,500-plus acres of terrain is more than Breckenridge has on three peaks. Yet only two chairlifts are needed

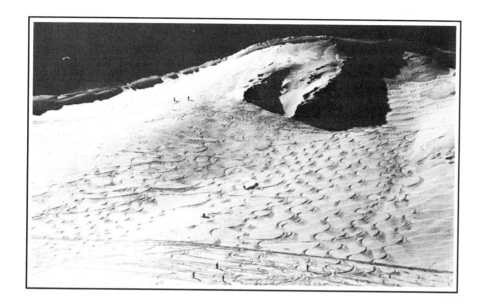

With 3,100 vertical feet and over thirty lifts, Mammoth Mountain lives up to its name.

to access most of Targhee's wide bowls, fairytale glades, and intermittent ridges. (A novice chair and a kiddie tow are also found near the base.) The mountain is sublimely intermediate—70 percent solid blue square, and the conditions usually are A-1. The base development—two small lodges, a handful of condominiums, and service buildings—is too modest to be called a real village. Yet such amenities as a restaurant, bar, cafeteria, heated outdoor pool, and super-size hot tub exist and they do suffice. The enforced intimacy, the low prices, and the reliable snow combine to make Targhee a most unusual little resort.

MAMMOTH MOUNTAIN/JUNE MOUNTAIN, CALIFORNIA

Rarely has a ski mountain been as appropriately named as Mammoth. This behemoth is a giant by any measure: 3,100 vertical feet, thirty lifts (including two gondolas and four quads), more than a hundred wide slopes, humongous bowls, tree-lined trails, and a mind-blowing uphill capacity of 42,000 skiers an hour—roughly as much as Snowmass and Keystone combined. Mammoth skis big—and Mammoth skis long. Spring is the favorite time for Los Angeles skiers, for whom Mammoth is a distant but do-able weekend trip, and the season regularly stretches into July. Like other giants, Mammoth offers an abundance of every kind of terrain imaginable, from ballroom beginner slopes to wall-like ridges above treeline.

Added to Mammoth's magnitude is nearby June Mountain, purchased in 1986 with the expectation of eventually connecting the two with some sort of high-tech super-lift. June, with 2,590 vertical feet and over thirty runs, has traditionally been a quieter family area, half-an-hour by road from Mammoth's madding crowds. A high-speed tram opened for the 1987-88 season to ferry skiers from the parking lot to the lodge.

Limited mountain lodging is available, notably the Mammoth Inn and a relatively small number of condos—relative, that is, to the accommodations for 30,000 at Mammoth Lakes. The closest lodging to June Mountain is at June Lakes, which can house 20,000. Both are year-round resort communities with tons of places to sleep, eat, and party. Mammoth, as the more popular target of young skiers, is the more action-packed town, especially on weekends.

MOUNT BACHELOR, OREGON

When newspaper sports stories appear, quoting a U.S. Ski Team coach or racer and carrying a Bend, Oregon, dateline, they're really talking Mount Bachelor. Looming over central Oregon's high desert, Bachelor has long been a team favorite, for the ski season opens in November and winds down in July. From Memorial Day on, skiers share the Summit Chair with sightseers riding to enjoy the panoramic view—an odd sensation for anyone hardcore enough to ski in summer.

Bachelor, billing itself as "the mountain of the future," is breaking into the big time in a big way and may eventually force people to think of Oregon as ski country. The mountain resembles nothing so much as a squooshed-down Mount Fuji transformed from a place of pilgrimage to a place for skiing. Evenly shaped, with trees on the lower sections and a snow-capped, slightly flat-topped summit, its 3,100 vertical feet are served by two high-speed quads, a high-speed triple, and seven fixed-grip chairlifts. The overwhelming majority of the fifty-one marked runs offer ultra-pleasurable intermediate skiing. Bachelor has become a terrific learning center, with programs that include a three-day learn-to-ski guarantee and racing programs galore. Accommodations from deluxe resorts to economical motels are available in and near Bend, twenty-two scenic miles away.

PURGATORY, COLORADO

Purgatory is heaven for skiers who have discovered this rapidly growing resort in southwestern Colorado. Known for abundant acres of easy slopes and pleasure-cruising terrain on a 2,022-foot vertical, Purgatory really began to shine with its 1985-86 expansion into The Legends, 150 acres of steady fall-line powder slopes for advanced and expert skiers. Subsequently, Purgatory became one of the first in the West to purchase a winch cat, the newest high-tech, high-priced toy which permits grooming the heretofore ungroomable steeps. Portions of The Legends have now been turned into something even more heavenly for those who like their runs both super-steep and super-smooth.

Condos provide slopeside lodging for more than 2,000 skiers, and there is dining, entertainment, and shopping in a modern little village. A wider range, including the delightfully Victorian Strater Hotel, once a favorite of author Louis L'Amour, is offered at Durango, a traditional western town twenty-five miles away. Tamarron, between the town and the mountain, is one of the country's premier full-service, self-contained resorts.

Heli-Skiing

HELI-SKIING IS THE RISKIEST
OF ALL SKI ADVENTURES
ORDINARILY AVAILABLE

Throughout history, mountains have inspired awe in mortals. Gods have dwelt on peaks from Mount Olympus to Mount Fuji. Indian mystics and Greek monks inhabit lonely mountain caves, and crucifixes appear on the highest points of the Alps. Yet skiers, earthbound by the lifts which take them to the mountaintops and the routes prescribed for their descent, sometimes lose the mountains' sense of majesty. That is, perhaps, one reason for the surging popularity of heli-skiing. To have done it lifts ordinary skiers into a select fraternity of perhaps 15,000.

The Canadian Rockies seem to have been made for heli-skiing. They are remote and rugged with untold acres of high-mountain parkland spread over thousands of square miles. The timberline is at just 7,000—3,000 feet lower than the U.S. Rockies. Mile upon mile of high peaks, gentle glaciers, splendid meadows, and densely treed forests of fir or larch are blanketed in white powder. But powder is just one of the snow conditions you may encounter during any given run, which may include mashed potatoes, windpack, breakable crust, the rubble of an old avalanche, and corn snow, in season or not.

Powder is the ideal, but the satisfaction comes in having encountered it all—and skied it all.

In order to ride in the helicopters, skiers divide up into small groups.

Heli-skiing is more than the ultimate skiing experience, it is also a lifestyle—one that sprang from the fantasy of an Austrian mountaineer named Hans Gmoser. In the sixties, Gmoser began scouting ski runs in what are known as the "interior ranges" of eastern British Columbia with the notion of bringing small groups of elite skiers in by helicopter. In 1965, he led just eight sturdy skiers to the first heli-skiing adventures in the Bugaboos, a range that has become a virtual synonym for heli-skiing. In 1968 Gmoser built the Bugaboo Lodge—not lushly luxurious but very comfortable—to house, feed, and amuse forty-four skiers. The number was not arbitrarily chosen. A busload of forty-four skiers breaks down into four groups of eleven—each of which, plus a guide, just fills a Bell 212 twin-engine chopper.

It wasn't long before every skier had at least heard about heli-skiing—and many longed to try it. Over the next fifteen years, new, increasingly posh lodges were built by Gmoser and his company, Canadian Mountain Holidays (CMH), in the Cariboos and the Bobbie Burns. A camp for workers at a remote hydro plant was upgraded and used for skiing the Monashees, the most challenging of the ranges where CMHers ski. Motels are used in Valemount and Revelstoke, and daytrips are run out of Panorama, a medium-size resort with modern accommodations. In 1987, CMH began operations in the Gothics, a range noted for wide open slopes as well as dense forests, from a complex of prefab structures originally erected to house copper miners and quickly nicknamed "Ice Station Zebra" by heli-skiers.

CMH, based in Banff, Alberta, though operating across the provincial line in British Columbia, inevitably inspired a series of imitative operations—Rudi Gertsch's Mountain Canada, based in Golden, British Columbia, and operating in the Purcell and Selkirk Ranges; and Mike Wiegele Helicopter Skiing, also out of Banff, with skiing in the Monashees and the Cariboos. More outfits have begun heli-skiing by the day: Banff Heli-Sports based in Banff, Alberta; Whistler Heli-Ski based at Whistler Village; Kootenay Heli-Ski out of Nakusp; and Selkirk-Tangiers Heli-Skiing operating from Golden—all in British Columbia. The fever has spread to the United States too, notably Colorado First Tracks Helicopter Powder Guides in Aspen; Mammoth Heli-Ski at Mammoth Lakes, California; Ruby Mountain Heli-Ski in Lemoille, Nevada; Sun Valley Helicopter Ski Guides in Idaho; and Wasatch Powderbird Guides at Snowbird, Utah.

Yet the essence of heli-skiing is to make a week of it in western Canada, preferably with CMH, which developed a ritual that has become legendary. The group for each specific destination forms up at Calgary airport for a bus ride to the staging area for shuttle flights deep into the mountains. There is cheer and fear, merriment and introspection, exhilaration and anticipation as the skiers— normally an international lot comprised of North Americans, Europeans, South Americans, and perhaps a sprinkling from British Commonwealth outposts—sort themselves out. Who has heli-skied before? Where? How good are the best skiers? How weak are the worst? They should all be strong advanced skiers and must be capable of handling various kinds of snow under a variety of conditions. Most people who sign up are at least that capable, and after going through all that trouble and expense, few have chickened out and quit. (To appeal to those put off by the mucho-macho reputation of heli-skiing, however, there are now less strenuous introductory weeks.) The mix is mostly male and usually heavy on the shady side of forty, the peak-earning-years generation for whom this most expensive ski vacation is an affordable dream.

Last week's group is flown out as this week's is flown in. Rumors are exchanged. What was the weather like? The snow? How many vertical feet were skied? One hundred thousand is considered a good week. The record is double that.

The next morning virtually shimmers with excitement. Powdersuits are donned. The bindings of special soft-flexing powder skis are adjusted. Avalanche drills are practiced. Beepers the size of small transistor radios are passed out, and everyone listens intently to the briefing on their use. These transceivers, worn deep under layers of clothing, are to be kept on "transmit" all day. In the event of a slide, they emit signals that will help locate buried skiers. Those not swept under the snow are taught how to turn the units to "receive" and to begin searching. The guide, selfishly as well as professionally, wants to be sure everyone understands the drill, for he is often in front of the group, and in case of a slide, most likely to be caught. Slides are not a frivolous concern, for heli-skiing is the riskiest of all ski adventures ordinarily available. Despite the precautions developed over the years and the skills and savvy of the certified, superlatively trained cadre of guides, there have been thirty-six heli-skiing fatalities since the first one in 1972.

Perhaps the knowledge of the danger adds an extra tingle to the palpable excitement of that first morning. The adrenaline flows hard as the helicopter arrives and the group crawls toward it, keeping low to stay clear of the blades which whirl loudly yet invisibly overhead. The guide stacks the skis aboard, and the helicopter lifts off. It's an eerie feeling, even for those with many hours in airplanes, to climb straight up and bank sharply without wings to buoy the machine. The pilots don't need to fly high. It seems as if you could reach out and touch a canyon wall, and you wonder if the trees are tickling the bird's undercarriage. In a few minutes, you land, perhaps on an impossible tiny pinnacle. The skiers tumble out quickly, crouching low, and kneel in a circle. It's the "heli-huddle," another of the rituals with which one so quickly becomes familiar. Then the helicopter lifts off to fetch the next group. Perhaps they are of a different skill level and will be skiing elsewhere, or perhaps they'll land where you did. But even then, they may be using a different route or will be just far enough behind you that you won't see them until teatime back at the lodge.

And that's where the essence of the mountains comes in: everything is a million miles away,

Satisfaction comes from conquering all types of snow.

and you and a small group of comrades who quickly become friends are alone on top of the world. Occasionally, the place and conditions are such that the guide will let everyone loose to dance through the perfect powder of the ultimate snowfield. More often, he will poke around in the snow, ski a few hundred feet this way or that, and move with deliberateness that can be reassuring or frustrating, depending on your point of view, before giving the signal for the rest of the group to ski. He will plow through the snow, a vision of grace and power, seemingly oblivious to a fifty-pound pack on his back. The group may be asked to follow his tracks exactly, to ski one by one, or be given a set of boundaries—perhaps from "the middle of that ridge to the left to a line with that boulder on the right," or farther down, "a straight line up from those two trees." In this world of limitless snow, the guide sets the limits.

Thus the day progresses—and so the week. The heli-skiing operators, who must pay a permit fee for each run they utilize, have had to name the nameless snowfields and couloirs, headwalls and glades in order to make the bureaucrats' lives easier. Depending on where you're skiing, the runs down Powder Pig or Kissing Dogs, the Vowell Glacier or the Molloy Icefield, Snow Ocean or Bill's Pass follow one another—two thousand vertical feet here, three and a half thousand there. There are on-the-spot box lunches on high plateaus. The sun may be as strong and hot as on Maui, or the air so cold that the departing chopper will flash-freeze your sandwich. Only two things are predictable: one is that you can't rely on the snow or weather, and the other is that it will be the adventure of a lifetime.

Heli-skiing is demanding, yet it is not the same type of skiing provided by a hard day at a lift-served ski area with no lines. There's no non-stop up and down, for heli-skiing is a deliberate activity. There's waiting time while the guide tests the snow, or while a skier extricates himself from a tree well, or while another retrieves his skis, poles, goggles, and hat scattered by the kind of wipe-out that heli-skiers refer to as a "garage sale." There is the sensual pleasure of skiing fresh powder as well as you can. There is the challenge of snow conditions that aren't so idyllic—and the satisfaction that comes from having triumphed over them. You've met the mountain on its own terms, and you've adjusted to its demands in a harmony that astonishes even the most jaded skiers. Perhaps most enduringly, there's the rare and matchless combination of solitude and camaraderie. While moving, the changing conditions remind you that this is skiing in the rough, skiing on snow the way nature put it down in the wilderness. While waiting, the majesty of the mountains is overwhelming.

Back in the lodge, over beer or brandy, both satisfaction and awe translate into a display of bragging rights over which group skied the hardest, which got in the most vertical feet, or which produced the most spectacular crashes.

The days laze by out of range of television or newspapers, beyond the reach of the telephone for any but the most dire crisis. If it's too stormy for flying, there may be a day of Scrabble or saunas, snowball fights or drinking contests. And when the clouds blow away, there might be a couple of feet of new powder just waiting to be skied—paradise in western Canada. The week's end suddenly dawns with crashing reality. The group, which became so quickly and intimately acquainted, will soon dissolve. Participants begin totalling up their verticals—and those with several weeks and a milestone of a million vertical feet, or multiples thereof, smilingly accept their awards. Vows are made to meet again, perhaps same time, next year. The helicopter lands beside the lodge. A group of initiates, glowing with expectation, disembarks. The veterans—so wise, so experienced, so happy, so tired—climb aboard. The torch passes, but the flame rekindled by so special an experience burns on.

Lake Louise, Sunshine & Banff, Alberta

LOCATED NEXT TO THE HELI-SKIING
CAPITAL OF THE WORLD, THESE
LIFT-SERVED AREAS OFFER THE
EPITOME OF HIGH MOUNTAIN SKIING

The town of Banff is an island of summer tourism in the sea of mountains that is Canada's Banff National Park. Banff Avenue is lined with shops specializing in Scottish tartans and English bone china, and the surrounding neighborhood is residential. It seems an unlikely ski resort. The baronial Banff Springs Hotel, looming like a Brobdingagian castle over a community suddenly reduced to Lilliput, is like nothing in the skiing world short of The Palace in Gstaad. This hotel, one of the celebrated grand resorts built by the Canadian Pacific Railroad in the Gilded Age, feels too elegant to be a ski lodge. By contrast, the town's motels and lodges seem laid out to accommodate the summer tourists' motorcoaches. Banff's ski connection looks tenuous.

But that's only until you stand on the edge of a precipitous slope atop Mt. Norquay watching local youngsters yodel down the bumps. Or until—after a long trip on a slow chairlift, followed by a platterpull, and finally a climb of a few hundred feet—you arrive at the top of the Lake Louise

*Built by the Canadian Pacific Railroad,
the Banff Springs Hotel is a turreted landmark.*

Ski Area and marvel at the sudden splendor of tree-free back bowls unfolding before you. Or until you disembark from the two-and-a-half-mile-long access gondola that has ferried you and your luggage to Sunshine Village, a tiny resort in a high bowl, which you will share with fewer than two hundred other overnight guests. Then Banff suddenly, and rightly, joins the ranks of big-league skiing.

Located in the heart of the Canadian Rockies, these three—Mt. Norquay, Lake Louise, and Sunshine—are the nearest lift-served ski areas to the celebrated peaks of the Bugaboos, Monashees, and Cariboos, which comprise the world's heli-skiing capital. Norquay is Banff's hometown hill, all-too-often untested by visitors. Its night-skiing lights glow at the eastern edge of town. Sunshine (ten miles from Banff) and Lake Louise (thirty-eight miles away) compete both for ski vacationers and day skiers from Calgary. The trio offers an interchangeable lift ticket under the marketing umbrella of the Banff Club Ski. Forty-five minutes east of Banff is Nakiska at Mt. Allan, the 1988 Winter Olympic Alpine skiing venue.

LAKE LOUISE

Lake Louise is the biggest ski area in the Canadian Rockies and one of the largest in North America. Its vertical measures 3,250 feet—3,000 feet being the dividing line between big ski mountains and *really* big ski mountains. The main peak is Whitehorn, and the terrain visible from the bottom is a solid, densely wooded tract criss-crossed with meandering ski trails. At the base is a small beginner section and two chairlifts: the slow-moving Olympic chair and the newer Glacier double.

The front of the mountain is webbed with a dozen traditional trails, handsomely cut in the late sixties. Whitehorn has wide runs on which men's and women's World Cup downhill races are held, cutoffs through the trees, and moguled drop-offs that bring a tingle to the spine. But these features account for just a third of Lake Louise's offerings—in fact, the least interesting third.

The timberline, which is at 11,000 feet in Colorado, is at about 8,000 feet in Alberta, so Lake Louise's trees begin to thin out along the upper reaches of the chairlifts. The Summit platter drags skiers up a steep snowfield, open except for avalanche fences and outcroppings of rock.

The front face of the mountains is real Rockies, but the back—making up two-thirds of the terrain—is pure Alps. The Back Bowls area is a wondrous white world that epitomizes high-mountain skiing. Hotshots can drop off the summit into a choice of black-diamond chutes that widen into grand powder terrain after a snowfall, which otherwise are sensational mogul fields. Advanced skiers skirt an upper catwalk around the bowl until they find a less steep and more congenial ridge line or gully.

Most good skiers ride the Ptarmigan and Paradise chairs and stay in the Bowls all day—bumping down Ptarmigan Bowl, skiing the powder in Paradise Bowl, or shifting into overdrive on Brown Shirt. The Bowls even have two long roads marked with green circles. They should not be confused with the gentle novice slopes, similarly designated with green, at the Whitehorn base, for these back-of-mountain greens are the routes which solid intermediates take to yet another chairlift which, in turn, accesses a second peak called Larch. In 1954, when Larch was called Temple Mountain, a Pomalift was installed there, and the area was a good day's cross-country excursion from the nearest road. But in the eighties, new lift construction made Larch accessible to all. Larch has groomable trails cut straight and wide through thick forests. Blue squares predominate, and skiers with considerably less than expert skill and endurance can cruise all day.

The Back Bowls and Larch spill into the same high valley. Skiers from the two slopes share the Temple Lodge, an on-mountain cafeteria cum sundeck and barbecue for those mid-winter days when mild Chinook winds suddenly bring springtime to the Canadian Rockies.

LODGING AND ACTIVITIES

Many vacationers who ski the slopes of Lake Louise, of course, stay in Banff and commute the thirty-eight miles either by car or Banff Club Ski bus. Others overnight at the opulent Chateau Lake Louise only four miles away on the shores of Lake Louise. The Chateau, like the Banff Springs Hotel, was constructed by the railroad to draw summer visitors to the national park. It has been open during the winter since the late seventies. A 125-room addition, built in 1987, brings the total to five hundred rooms, all new or recently renovated. The nearby Deer Lodge, Lake Louise Inn, Post Hotel, and West Lake Louise Lodge are smaller, simpler accommodations, but the Chateau is the center of non-ski and après-ski life. Activities include cross-country skiing at a new touring center which gives lessons and runs wonderful excursions, horse-drawn sleigh rides, tobogganing on a special hill, and fun-filled fondue parties.

SUNSHINE

Skiers who love the look of Lake Louise's Back Bowls but prefer the pitch of the gentler Larch adore Sunshine, whose terrain combines the two. A mini-resort and a maxi-day-skiing area, Sunshine Village is a place apart. It is a tiny huddle of lodges pocketed in a high, treeless bowl with lifts practically at the door. Guests are joined on the slopes by day skiers, but when the ski tails of the last of them have wagged down the five-and-a-half mile run called the Bourgeau Express, the Village becomes a private corner of congeniality and a low-key night-time glimmer.

In 1934 the powder-laden bowl that is now Sunshine enticed a handful of pioneers who first skied out of a tiny cabin leased from the railroad. Four years later, when the cabin burned, a 720 square-foot log lodge replaced it, more than doubling the slopeside accommodations—from twelve bunks to thirty. The first official rope tow was installed in 1945, and in 1951, Brewster Transport began running buses up the mountain's multi-switchback access road. Chairlifts, T-bars, a ninety-room lodge, a day lodge, and finally a gondola followed at a deliberate pace.

From the village, at 7,082 feet, some lifts, including a new high-speed quad, climb to Mt. Standish and Lookout Mountain; others rise from the Lower Standish and Wheeler area. Standish is best in the morning sun, when its steep mogul slopes draw Sunshine's early birds. Dave Irwin, a member of the legendary wild Canadian downhill racing squad of the seventies and early eighties known on the World Cup circuit as the "Crazy Canucks," has now settled down as Sunshine's marketing director. To watch him skip down Standish's biggest moguls is to see that, contrary to stereotype, downhill racers *can* turn their skis.

SKIING

Lookout Mountain stands out far above the timberline. While it is just 1,800 feet higher than the Village, the endless mountain views and unimpeded slopes give it an expansiveness that belies its modest vertical. Lookout is largely a playground of great, tame snowfields and packed-down European-style *pistes*. But it also has near-vertical cornices, mogully headwalls, and steep faces with double fall lines to pack a double challenge into every turn. Lookout's outer limits are actually across the provincial border in British Columbia. No passports are necessary.

The border follows the Continental Divide, the dumping ground for snow both from Pacific and Plains storms, so Sunshine logs by far the highest average snowfall in the Banff region. While Lake Louise and Norquay average less than 150 inches of snow a year and have supplemental snowmaking systems, Sunshine receives 400 inches a year straight from heaven. As a result, the resort has the region's longest ski season—from mid-November until June.

Approved for future expansion but with no timetable firmed up is the development of Goat's Eye Mountain, a 2,200-foot canted ridge which could support three lifts and skiing both above and below the treeline.

LODGING

The Sunshine Inn is the heart of the resort where ski instruction, excellent food, and convivial après-ski combine into a total ski-vacation environment, and the old lodge, which the Inn replaces, is still in use as a brownbaggers' day lodge. The Inn now has been renovated, and Sunshine's plans call for up to three hundred luxurious apartment-style units to be added.

NORQUAY

Norquay, Banff's oldest ski area, was established in 1923. The present base lodge dates back to 1941, though of course it has been renovated. Its first chairlift, a single built in 1948, was the first chairlift in Canada. It has since been replaced by a double, but in the fifties, when the Tea Room summit lodge was built, every concrete mixer, sack of masonry materials, sheet of plywood, plank, board, beam, and plate-glass window rode uphill on that workhorse of a single chair.

SKIING

Norquay was built in an era when people seem to have been either novice skiers or very good ones. The ski area therefore has some very easy terrain, a lot of extremely challenging acreage, and little in between. Most skiers do not feel that 1,300 vertical feet merits a vacation day, but they are wrong. The mountain's steeps are a match for any in the Rockies. From the top of the Norquay chair, the view of Banff and of Mt. Rundle is spectacular, but many first-time Norquay skiers are too conscious of their fast-beating hearts to appreciate the scenery. Lone Pine, the most famous slope, falls away at an alarming average 38-degree pitch nearly 1,200 feet to the base lodge. It is named after a solitary pine tree near the bottom of the run, a welcome sight to skiers who have made it down this awesome steep.

It is rumored that an ancient record of more than fifty Lone Pine runs in one day was set by a stalwart whose name is lost to memory. But the area nourishes such achievements by rewarding skiers exhibiting both skill and stamina with a gold pin for twenty-seven runs (equal to 35,000 vertical feet), a silver for twenty-three runs, and a bronze for nineteen runs. Less famous, but not much easier, runs are North American, Bowl, and Upper Valley.

Norquay finally got the recognition it deserves—at least in a very elite part of the world skiing community—in January 1987, when it hosted the XIII Interski. This quadrennial event is a gathering of the top instructors from all the world's ski countries who demonstrate the latest version of their respective official ski-teaching progressions. It is known as the "instructors' Olympics" and has great cachet in the ski world.

LODGING AND ACTIVITIES

The town of Banff, like Jackson, Wyoming, is a major summer tourist destination. Banff Avenue, the main street, is lined with shops, restaurants, and lodgings. It is a street meant for strolling, casual browsing, or serious shopping. Banff Avenue hums well into the evening, as diners and après-skiers bundle up against the Canadian cold and head back to their lodgings.

To have everything on a grand scale and with much opulence under one roof, one has to visit the Banff Springs Hotel. Upon entering the QE2-size main lobby, the word "fun" does not immediately spring to mind. But this great turreted landmark has successfully struck a balance between tradition and skiers' demands and has, indeed, created an air of fun. The hotel, open in winter since 1969, is fully geared to skiers.

There's sweaty fun in the completely equipped health spa, with up-to-the-minute exercise equipment, saunas, and steamrooms. There's watery fun in the splendidly tiled indoor pool, the heated outdoor pool, and the rooftop whirlpool, as well as at the Upper Hot Springs with water piped in from nature's source. There's nighttime fun in The Works, a terrific disco where the dancing is great and where the house punch is scooped in automated ladles driven by a Rube Goldberg pulley system. There's raucous fun in Mt. Stephen's Hall where a rollicking Medieval Feast, presided over by a king and queen for the evening, is put on for ski clubs and groups. And there's cornpone fun at the hayride and barbecue, where dinner is a chow-down of famous Alberta beef cooked over an open-pit fire, followed by dancing to country-and-western tunes. And there's the extravagant fun of looking at, or buying, a diamond bracelet or a chinchilla wrap in one of the exclusive shops in the hotel's shopping arcade.

The great hotel's 525 guest rooms are furnished with lovely pieces and are thoroughly warm and charming. There are even spacious suites in the turrets and under the eaves where cramped staff and servants' rooms once were. The Tudor House and Banff Springs Hotel Manor are former staff houses, gutted in 1987 and turned into two hundred additional luxury units.

There are plenty of other accommodations in Banff. The Banff Park Lodge and Inns of Banff are both modern, well-appointed hotel complexes on the outskirts of town. The Rimrock Inn up near the hot springs has a grand view of Banff but is less formal than the Banff Springs Hotel. Budget watchers favor the King Edward Hotel and the Mt. Royal Hotel, both in the center of town.

RESTAURANTS

Alberta beef is justly famous, and the best of it can be found in the Banff Springs Hotel's Rob Roy Dining Room, Inns of Banff Park's Reflections Restaurant, and Bumpers Beef House downtown. But Banff offers more than great steak. Le Beaujolais has sophisticated tableside cooking and French cuisine. Giorgio's, Guido's, and Ticino are known for fine Italian fare, the last with a distinct Swiss-Italian accent. For more ethnicity and less formality, the Balkan specializes in Greek food and the Yard serves Tex-Mex dishes.

The best nightlife for après-skiers of all ages is at the Banff Springs Hotel and the Chateau Lake Louise. But the young crowd, whose music must be loud, shuttles between the bar at the King Eddie, Tommy's Steak Pit, and Fast Freddy's. Sidestreet is a good sports bar, the Magpie & Stump usually has folk music, and the View Point in the Rimrock is for easy listening.

Americans have perhaps been made more conscious of the Canadian Rockies by the 1988 Winter Olympics. For Canadian skiers, Banff is a popular winter choice, and even Japanese visitors have long made it their number-one destination in North America. They ski the mountains, load up on English tea cups, and drink in the splendor that is Banff. It's time more south-of-the-border skiers joined them.

Whistler & Blackcomb, British Columbia

THEY ARE THE ONLY SKI AREAS
IN NORTH AMERICA WITH
VERTICALS OF OVER 5,000 FEET

Whistler Mountain and Blackcomb, the only ski areas in North America with verticals of over 5,000 feet, are in British Columbia's Coastal Mountains. They share a valley, a village, a postal code. Two of their chairlifts have bottom stations a scant hundred yards apart. The concept is simply staggering—for the skiing isn't just statistically impressive—and the two ski areas are perfect counterpoints to each other.

Vancouver skiers, who drive less than two hours to reach Whistler Village, constantly discuss which mountain they prefer. Some opt for the rolling, turning, variable-pitch runs of Whistler, while others prefer the predictable fall-line skiing of Blackcomb. Vancouverites may debate the two mountains' merits over a glass of Molson's, but most visitors don't find one "better" than the other—just different. Whistler, the older ski area, is a complex multi-faced piece of topography that is covered with a scattershot lift network and a lacework of trails. The lower portion of this hulking *massif* has heavily forested terrain made up of headwalls, plateaus, ridgelets, and knobs.

There are plenty of double-black-diamond runs that are an exhilarating delight for experts.

The ski runs weave among every type of crease, fold, and outcropping the mountain has to offer. Blackcomb, by contrast, presents one skiable face, with a parallel set of steady fall-line runs down the huge vertical. Whistler is complicated. Blackcomb is straightforward. Both offer glorious glacial snowfields for year-round skiing and five-mile top-to-bottom runs.

Skiers use one fully interchangeable lift pass to move freely between the two for a combination of vertical and variety that is unequalled in North America. By participating in a fast-paced Club Esprit week, intermediate and advanced skiers are led to the powder pockets, secret glades, and incredible steeps—and improve their skiing as well.

SKIING

Whistler has two ports of entry. On the south, the main lift from the original base is a twenty-three-year-old, four-passenger gondola that moves at a pace which can charitably be called stately. (It takes thirty-two minutes via gondola plus chairlift to get to the Roundhouse, a busy day lodge perched on a plateau which is the on-mountain hub of Whistler activity.) Starting in 1988-89, a new high-speed gondola goes from the edge of Whistler Village on the north side to the Roundhouse in seventeen minutes. The continent's only ten-passenger lift, it is one of two standup gondolas built during the summer of 1988 (Stratton, Vermont, has the other).

Below the Roundhouse, two dozen or so trails are marked on the map but a far greater choice of routes exists, for this mountain has merges, convenient cross-overs, small connectors, and major intersections so that, in a hundred runs, the mountain can be skied a hundred different ways—and that's just if you ski the cut trails. When you include the limitless powder routes amid the lush stands of trees, the choice is infinite. Seven lifts service this part of the area. The Village and Olympic chairs are sequential access lifts from Whistler Village. The rest are the color-name lifts: Olive, Red, and Little Red serving mostly intermediate and advanced trails on the gondola side; Black, appropriately, used mostly for bump runs like Raven, Zeppo's, and Tokum; and the Green chairs for wide, winning beginner and intermediate terrain. The Blue chair starts just above the Roundhouse and finishes below it, primarily serving a trio of wide, steep runs that draw powder skiers like a magnet draws iron filings—and, when the powder has been skied off, these runs bump up into sensational mogul pitches.

Whistler's true splendor, however, lies in five great bowls, one a glacier, that form a pristine semi-circle above the Roundhouse. Three lifts access this tree-free high-mountain paradise. On snowy days, experts impatiently make do on the Blue and Little Red chairs until the Patrol is ready to open the bowls. The Peak chair services Whistler and West bowls, which are, unquestionably, expert areas. Sheer cornices, steep snowfields, and sets of chutes with alarming pitches become powdery playgrounds. Also off the Peak chair is Glacier Bowl. Tamer terrain, it is the site of the Dave Murray Summer Ski Camp and the Canadian Ski Team's summer training center.

When skiers ride the parallel T-bars to the Glacier outrun or to Harmony Bowl, they might be in the Alps. With two surface lifts jutting off toward a razorback ridge on a treeless horizon, one sees a picture that is the essence of high-mountain, Alpine skiing. Harmony is an interesting and varied bowl, which offers excellent advanced skiing, along with a few routes for high-intermediate skiers. Beyond is Burnt Stew Basin, a thousand pristine acres—the size of Harmony, Whistler, and

Glacier combined—added to Whistler's in-bounds terrain in 1987-88. Eventually, there will be a lift in Burnt Stew, which will eliminate the current circuit via the Blue chair and T-bars. The lift, not yet configured precisely, would increase Whistler's total vertical from its current 5,006 feet.

Neighboring Blackcomb has North America's highest vertical. Its terrain also has two entrance points, but in contrast to Whistler's multi-directional sprawl, Blackcomb has developed only one side of its mountain. The Fitzsimmons chair is the one that originates next to Whistler's Village chair. The other entry point is at Blackcomb's growing and developing main base. The Wizard Express, which is one of three high-speed quads, whisks skiers toward the sky. On the lower part of the mountain there are a dozen intermediate runs including little side trails and cut-offs. Future expansion in this section of the mountain will add novice and intermediate runs just north of the current trail network, and more intermediate and a few advanced runs on the Whistler side.

Blackcomb, however, begins to get very interesting at its middle level, where short, tricky black-diamond pitches and lose-yourself-in-the-trees-and-don't-come-out-till-spring glades can be found. The Solar Coaster Express and the Stoker triple serve this sector, where Blackcomb's terrain, so contained near the base, begins to fan out. The Jersey Cream chair leads to half-a-dozen north-facing expert runs and the tight, snow-holding glades between them.

As Whistler has the Roundhouse near timberline, Blackcomb's similarly situated Rendezvous Restaurant is its mountain hub. While Whistler's bowls begin as an arc around the Roundhouse, Blackcomb's are tucked behind the summit, nicknamed Mile High Station, for it is precisely 5,280 vertical feet from the bottom of the Wizard Express. Bowl skiing is heavenly, as indicated by the name of its new topside quad, the Seventh Heaven Express. Catwalks lead right and left from the top of the chair. The right one skims the top of Lakeside Bowl, which starts as an ultra-wide, moderately pitched slope before separating into undulating trails. Farther along, the slope steepens and ultimately offers the option of great tree skiing. In 1988, a catwalk was added to access the 240 acres of high-mountain skiing on Blackcomb Glacier.

But it is the left side that presents the greatest challenge. A short catwalk leads to the medium-steep Horstman Glacier—which offers summer skiing—and then the catwalk eventually leads to Blackcomb and Secret Bowls. These are not wide bowls for ego skiing but are scrunched into deep, high-walled troughs riddled with narrow, rock-rimmed chutes that tax the psyche as well as the body. Double black diamonds prevail. Perhaps a category of triple black should be created for the anorexically skinny chutes threaded through rock cliffs. The most famous is the Saudan Couloir, a near free fall, appropriately named after France's fabled skier of the steep, Sylvain Saudan.

On Easter weekend, Blackcomb puts on the Ski Race Extreme, exceptionally demanding in terms of skill, stamina, and sheer guts. It starts with a courageous leap into Saudan's 42-degree opening pitch. Ultra-steep and extra-narrow, it is, of course, ungroomable. Competitors soon carve mega-ruts, ten to fifteen feet deep, in the soft snow. The course then looks like a giant luge run. Further down the bowl widens a lot and gentles a little, before skiers are rocketed onto the hard-pack of Jersey Cream. Twenty-five hundred vertical feet from the start, the survivors ski, exhausted, through the finish line.

HISTORY

What is now the Whistler area has been hosting visitors for decades, though its skiing is much more recent. In 1914, Myrtle and Alex Philips built Rainbow Lodge on Alta Lake, one of five pristine lakes in the mountains north of Squamish. Early on the area was a popular honeymoon resort. Canoeing down the River of Golden Dreams was beautiful and romantic. After World War II, however, a group of skiers, dissatisfied with the marginal skiing closer in to Vancouver, decided to build a new ski area. Inspired by the isolated 1960 Winter Olympic site of Squaw Valley, they hired the late Willy Schaeffler, who had designed Squaw, as a consultant.

After London Mountain was found to be suitable, a group of Vancouver businessmen created a lift company, caused a road to be built, and cut the mountain's first trails. Renamed Whistler after the danger signal emitted by indigenous marmots, the ski mountain opened in 1965, and its success spurred building in the valley. Though much of the early development was haphazard, by the time investors were ready to build a major resort village in the late seventies, a firm master plan for the area was in place and strictly enforced. The new village would combine Old World charm and New World practicality. In the European mode, buildings were required to be harmonious yet varied, and view corridors from the central plaza to the mountains were to be retained. In the North American mode, plenty of underground parking was mandated. The effect, as planned, is both attractive and functional.

The year 1980 was pivotal. Construction on the Village escalated, the Whistler lift company was sold to new investors, who immediately built three chairs on the north side, and Blackcomb Mountain was opened, a flattering reflection of Whistler's success. With its roots in the sixties, Whistler had grown in spurts. As a ski area of the eighties, Blackcomb opened with a planned trail system on a huge vertical. Five years later, Blackcomb put in the Seventh Heaven T-bar, giving it North America's longest lift-served vertical. Whistler countered in 1987 with the Peak chair, nudging its vertical over the 5,000-foot mark. In 1987, Blackcomb spent $25 million on improvements including its three quads, until then the biggest single-season expansion on the continent. Whistler again quickly parried by announcing its $18.5 million gondola. During the 1987-88 season, both ski areas again changed hands.

LODGING

There are accommodations, mostly condominiums and private homes operating like European-style pensions, up and down the valley, but *the* place to stay is Whistler Village, where everything is within easy walking distance of the lifts. In fact, from the Carleton Lodge condos, you can practically roll out of bed and onto the lifts. The Fireplace Inns, a fine condo-hotel just steps away, has private balconies, saunas, and whirlpools as well. The Delta Mountain Inn is the resort's largest, with some rooms offering private saunas or Jacuzzis. Nancy Greene's Olympic Lodge is a special place. The ebullient racer who won the first two overall titles in World Cup history, as well as two Olympic medals in 1968, now runs a modern hotel with a traditional atmosphere. A great career's worth of trophies shine from cases in the lobby, and her smile sparkles as she mingles with her guests—in the hotel and on the slopes as well, for taking a run with the champion innkeeper is one of the treats.

Another village-style development—as yet unnamed—is taking shape at the base of Blackcomb. And in 1989 the Chateau Whistler Resort will be completed. A CP Hotel (the chain runs such palatial places as the Banff Springs Hotel and Chateau Lake Louise), the $50 million, four-hundred-room facility will feature indoor and outdoor pools, indoor tennis, and other luxury amenities.

DINING AND APRÈS-SKI

Thirty years ago there was no paved road to the area, and a decade ago Whistler Village was just taking shape. But now it has real gastronomic highpoints, many run by expatriate chefs from Vancouver. Araxi's serves a changing potpourri of international dishes from Cajun to continental. Chez Joel's is run by Joel Thibault, a Frenchman who specializes in the Alpine cuisine of the Savoie region and Switzerland. Other Europeans, German-born Herb Neimann and Austrian-born Monika and Curt Czerveziak, offer the fare of their countries at their respective restaurants, the Black Forest Steak and Schnitzel House and Isabelle's. Sushi Village is a good Japanese restaurant. And Twigs does saucily special things with seafood.

Vigorous après-ski starts with a beer at the Longhorn and Nasty Jack's at the base of the lifts, while Nancy's Piano Bar, the International, and Citta are quieter spots. After dinner, the Savage Beagle gets a big, youthful crowd. Club Ten is a rowdy disco, while Barry T's has a quirky blue-collar ambiance and a good disco. Buffalo Bill's is a little older and dressier. Darts, video games, and other diversions are available at Tapley's Neighborhood Pub, and youngsters have their own après-ski spot at Whistler Wonderland, a popular arcade.

OTHER ACTIVITIES

Fifteen kilometers of track-set cross-country trails are accessible from the village, and forty-eight kilometers are at the Mad River Nordic Centre, fifteen miles to the south. The valley's five lakes are cleared for skating, and guided snowmobile tours to Cougar Lake are offered. Heli-skiing may be booked through three local operators. The Pumphouse is a fully-equipped fitness center, while Whistler Workout runs weekend and evening aerobics and exercise classes.

The Whistler/Blackcomb area offers world-class skiing, terrific accommodations, and ever-better village amenities, a scant and scenic seventy miles from Vancouver.

SUMMARY OF MOUNTAIN STATISTICS

Resort	Tram	Gondola	HS4C	FG4C	3C	2C	SL	Skiers/ Hour	Vertical Feet	Annual Snowfall	Skiable Acreage	Snowmaking	Longest Run	General Information	Snow Reports	Lodging Reservations
UNITED STATES																
California																
Tahoe Resorts														Greater Lake Tahoe Chamber of Commerce 916/583-2371		
Alpine Meadows	0	0	0	0	2	9	2	15,000	1,797	350″	2,000	4%	2.5 mi.	916/583-4242	916/583-6914	800/822-5959
Heavenly Valley	1	0	1	0	7	9	6	30,000	3,600	400″	N.A.	40%	5.5 mi.	916/541-1330	916/541-7544	800/822-5922
Kirkwood	0	0	0	0	4	6	1	15,000	2,000	450″	2,000	none	2.5 mi.	209/258-6000	209/258-3000	209/258-7247
Northstar	0	1 (4)	0	0	3	5	2	13,100	2,200	400″	1,700	1,000 ft.	2.9 mi.	916/562-1010	916/562-1330	800/824-8516
Squaw Valley	1	1 (6)	2	0	5	16	2	39,380	2,850	450″	8,300	none	3 mi.	916/583-6985	916/583-6955	800/824-7954
Colorado														Colorado/Ski Country/USA 303/837-0793		
Aspen Resorts																
Aspen Highlands	0	0	0	0	0	9	2	10,000	3,800	300″	515	10%	3.5 mi.	303/925-5300	303/925-5300	800/262-7736
Aspen Mountain	0	1 (6)	1	2	0	4	0	10,775	3,267	300″	625	35%	3 mi.	303/925-1220	303/925-1221	800/262-7736
Buttermilk	0	0	0	0	0	6	0	6,297	2,030	300″	402	30%	3 mi.	303/925-1220	303/925-1221	800/262-7736
Snowmass	0	0	3	0	2	9	2	20,535	3,615	300″	1,582	4%	3.7 mi.	303/925-2085	303/925-1221	800/332-3245
Ski The Summit Resorts														Summit County Chamber of Commerce 303/668-5800		
Arapahoe Basin	0	0	0	0	1	4	0	6,200	1,670	360″	350	none	1.5 mi.	303/468-2316	303/468-4111	800/222-0188
Breckenridge	0	0	3	0	1	9	1	22,050	2,610	255″	1,500	30%	3 mi.	303/453-2368	900/410-SNOW	303/453-2918
Copper Mountain	0	0	1	0	6	9	4	22,325	2,760	255″	1,180	25%	2.8 mi.	303/968-2882	303/962-2882	800/525-3828
Keystone	0	1 (6)	0	0	1	8	2	13,400	2,340	200″	680	75%	3 mi.	303/468-2316	303/369-6655	800/222-0188
Steamboat	0	1 (8)	0	1	7	10	2	29,000	3,600	325″	2,500	14%	3 mi.	303/879-6111	303/879-7300	303/879-0740
Telluride	0	0	1	0	2	6	1	10,836	3,155	300″	735	20%	2.85 mi.	303/728-3856	303/728-3614	800/525-3455
Vail Valley Resorts																
Beaver Creek	0	0	1	0	5	3	0	15,209	3,340	300″	800	25%	2.75 mi.	303/949-5750	303/476-4888	800/525-2257
Vail	0	1 (6)	6	1	3	9	2	35,600	3,100	325″	3,787	10%	4 mi.	303/476-5601	303/476-4888	800/525-3875
Winter Park	0	0	0	3	3	12	0	24,270	2,220	271″	1,105	5%	3.9 mi.	303/726-5514	303/726-4101	800/453-2525
Idaho																
Sun Valley																
Bald Mountain	0	0	3	0	6	3	0	19,844	3,400	250″	1,275	20%	3 mi.	208/622-4111	800/635-4150	800/635-4156
Dollar Mountain	0	0	0	0	1	2	0	4,800	628							
Maine																
Sugarloaf/USA	0	1 (4)	0	2	1	7	5	16,000	2,637	166″	300	75%	3 mi.	207/237-2000	207/237-2000	800/451-0002
New Hampshire																
Ski 93 Resorts																
Bretton Woods	0	0	0	0	1	2	1	4,600	1,500	180″	160	90%	2 mi.	603/278-5000	603/278-5051	603/278-1000
Cannon Mountain	1	0	0	0	1	2	3	6,730	2,146	156″	130	60%	2.33 mi.	603/823-5563	603/823-7771	603/823-5661
Loon Mountain	0	1 (4)	0	0	2	5	1	10,000	2,100	125″	234	80%	3 mi.	603/745-8111	603/745-8100	800/227-4191
Tenney Mountain	0	0	0	0	1	1	2	2,600	1,400	140″	186	90%	1.75 mi.	603/536-1717	800/222-2SKI	800/222-2SKI
Waterville Valley																
Mt. Tecumseh	0	0	1	0	3	4	3	N.A.	1,815	140″	225	85%	3 mi.	603/236-8311	603/236-4144	800/258-8988
Snow's Mountain	0	0	0	0	0	1	0									

Lifts

Resort	Tram	Gondola	HS4C	FG4C	3C	2C	SL	Skiers/ Hour	Vertical Feet	Annual Snowfall	Skiable Acreage	Snowmaking	Longest Run	General Information	Snow Reports	Lodging Reservations
New Mexico																
Taos Ski Valley	0	0	0	0	1	6	2	7,260	2,612	325″	1,000	5%	5.25 mi.	505/776-2291	505/776-2291	800/992-SNOW
Utah														Ski Utah 801/534-1779		
Little Cottonwood Canyon Resorts																
Alta	0	0	0	0	0	8	3	8,500	2,050	500″	1,700	none	3.5 mi.	801/742-3333	801/572-3939	801/742-2040
Snowbird	1	0	0	0	0	7	0	8,810	3,100	500″	1,900	none	3.3 mi.	801/742-2222	801/742-2222	800/453-3000
Park City (Parley's Canyon) Resorts														Park City Resort Chamber 800/453-1360		
Deer Valley	0	0	0	0	7	1	0	13,500	2,200	300″	750	9%	1.4 mi.	801/649-1000	801/649-2000	800/453-3833
Park City	0	1 (4)	0	0	5	8	0	18,700	3,100	350″	2,200	16%	3.5 mi.	801/649-8111	801/649-9571	800/367-3736
ParkWest	0	0	0	0	0	7	0	6,700	2,200	300″	850	30%	2.5 mi.	801/649-5400	801/649-5400	800/392-WEST
Vermont														Vermont Ski Areas Association 802/223-2439		
Killington	0	1 (4)	2	2	4	7	2	30,827	3,175	228″	721	N.C.	10.2 mi.	802/422-3333	802/422-3261	802/773-0755
Stowe														802/253-7311	802/253-8521	800/24-STOWE
Mt. Mansfield	0	1 (4)	1	0	1	2	0	5,170	2,350	250″	385	54%	4.5 mi.			
Spruce Peak	0	0	0	0	0	4	0	3,810	1,550							
Wyoming																
Jackson Hole	1	0	0	1	1	5	1	9,700	4,139	450″	2,500	5%	7 mi.	307/733-2292	307/733-2291	800/443-6931
CANADA																
Alberta																
Banff Resorts														Banff Club Ski 800/661-1431		
Lake Louise	0	0	0	0	2	4	3	12,180	3,250	185″	N.A.	N.C.	5 mi.	403/256-8473	403/244-6665	800/661-1158
Mt. Norquay	0	0	0	0	0	2	4	4,000	1,300	140″	130	35%	1.75 mi.	403/762-4421	403/253-3383	N.A.
Sunshine	0	1 (6)	0	0	1	5	5	13,900	3,497	300″	780	none	5 mi.	403/762-6500	403/227-7669	800/661-1363
British Columbia																
Whistler Village Resorts														Whistler Resort Association 604/932-3928		
Blackcomb	0	0	3	0	5	1	3	20,080	5,280	450″	1,600	Lower slopes	5 mi.	604/932-3141	604/932-4211	604/932-3650
Whistler Mountain	0	2 (10&4)	0	0	4	7	4	18,800	5,006	450″	2,148	Lower slopes	5 mi.	604/932-3434	604/932-4191	604/932-3650

* Key to lifts: Tram also called cable car (two large-capacity stand-up cars, one traveling up as the other travels downhill); Gondola, number in parentheses indicates how many places in each car; HS4C=high-speed detachable quad chair (super chair), number indicates how many such lifts; FG4C=fixed-grip quad chair; 3C=triple chair, number indicates how many such lifts; 2C=double chair, number indicates how many such lifts; SL=surface lifts, number indicates how many such lifts.

N.A.=Not available.

N.C.=Snowmaking exists but it has not been calculated in terms of square acres or as a percentage of total skiable acreage.

SUMMARY OF RESORT INFORMATION
THE BEST OF THE BEST
A Selection of the Best Lodging, Dining, and Diversions at the Best Ski Resorts in America

Resort	Lodging	Dining	Other
California Tahoe Resorts North Shore	Olympic Village Inn (Squaw) for convenience and luxury; Northstar condos for families; Truckee Hotel for traditional funk; River Ranch (Tahoe City) for service	Jakes-on-the-Lake (Tahoe City), seafood specialties; Christy Hill, fine dining; Squeeze Inn (Truckee), good omelettes	Grand, gaudy Vegas-style casinos in Reno; Circus Circus, tops for family fun
South Shore	Harvey's and Caesar's (Stateline), for flossy casino-hotel lodging; Ridge Tahoe (Heavenly Valley), luxurious condos with lift service to ski area	Christiania (Heavenly), for continental cuisine; Nephele's, for cocktails, a private hot tub, then steak dinner	Day-tripping to the North Shore aboard the "Tahoe Queen"
Colorado Aspen	Hotel Jerome, high-style Victorian; Hotel Lenado, small charming inn; Independence Square Hotel, great location, roof-top Jacuzzi; Little Red School Haus, top bargain lodge; Aspen Club, modern luxury and good health club	Guido's, terrific Italian; Sushi Masa, excellent Japanese; La Cocina and Toro's, reasonably priced Mexican	Wheeler Opera House, classical performances in an historic theater; shopping everywhere, après-ski, the Jerome Bar, Tippler's, and much more
Snowmass	Snowmass Club, spacious rooms, huge health spa; Stonebridge Inn, close to Mall and lifts; Woodrun Place, ski-in, ski-out luxury	Krabloonik, huskies in the pen, game specialties from the pan; Stew Pot, casual and reasonable	The Tower, après-ski magic; Snowmass Repertory Theater, peppy off-Broadway
Ski the Summit Breckenridge	Beaver Run, massive full-service resort; Village at Breckenridge, convenient to town and mountain; Fireside Inn, casual bargain inn	Spencer's, sleek and elegant; Briar Rose, charm; Polo Bar & Grille, beef bonanza	Tiger Run, snowmobile tours and rentals; après-ski at Colt's Sports Bar
Copper Mountain	Village Square, best-located condos; Club Med, only one at a US ski resort; Hyatt, watch for opening	The Plaza, eclectic gourmet menu; Rackets, modern health-food-style restaurant; Tuso's, best bar food	Copper Mountain Athletic Club, gorgeous spa center, especially the pool

Resort	Lodging	Dining	Other
Keystone	Keystone Lodge, first-rate services; Lancaster Lodge, new condo-hotel, walk to lifts; Ski Tip Lodge, traditional ski inn	Garden Room, Lodge's lush aerie, fine dining; Keystone Ranch, rustic elegance and fine fare; Old Dillon Inn, funky and Mexican	Cross-country excursions from touring center; indoor tennis; ice skating on Keystone Lake
Steamboat	Torian Plum, top condos; Bear Claw, ski-in, ski-out condos; Sheraton, full-service hotel; Harbor Hotel, well furnished in-town hotel; Vista Verde, distant but divine guest ranch; Scandinavian Lodge, traditional ambiance, ski into cross-country and downhill trail system	Mattie Silks, continental cuisine; Hazie's, lunch, dinner and best views; Giovanni's, hearty Italian; Cipriani's, elegant Italian	Ski tour at Rabbit Ears Pass; Tugboat, lively après-ski; SKID's Club, kids après-ski spot
Telluride	Lulu City and Etta Place, well-appointed condos; Dahl House, bargain guesthouse; New Sheridan, historic hotel, basic rooms	Julian's, fine northern Italian; Silverglade, mesquite magic; Sofio's, fun Mexican	Fly Me to the Moon Saloon, terrific après-ski and dance spot
Vail Valley Vail	Lodge at Vail, upscale elegance; Vail Athletic Club, fine rooms and spa; Westin, best full-service name-brand hotel; Gasthof Gramshammer, Austrian charm and matchless location; Sonnenalp, continental service and ambiance	Lord Gore, hearty fare; Ambrosia, continental elegance; Left Bank, French and fancy; Sweet Basil, good, fresh	Dobson Arena, skating, hockey; Vail Racquet Club, tennis and fitness; Colorado Ski Museum, fascinating; shopping in Vail Village
Beaver Creek	Centennial, The Charter, and Creekside, a trio of deluxe condos; Poste Montane, lavish condo-lodge	Beano's, private lunch club also offering not-to-be-missed sleigh and snow-coach dinners; The Legends, steak and seafood	Mountain-top ski-touring at McCoy Park; Drinkwater Park, lively après-ski
Winter Park	Iron Horse, lush condo-hotel; The Vintage, newest hotel; Gasthaus Eichler, new inn opened by popular restauranteurs; C Lazy U, leading dude ranch and touring center, worth the commute	The Slope and The Shed, busy après-ski and dining spots with varied menus; Gasthaus Eichler and Swiss Chalet, authentic European	The Stampede, aptly named for après-ski; only ski train in US, daily service from Denver
Idaho Sun Valley	Sun Valley Lodge, ski world classic; Sun Valley Inn, number two classic; Elkhorn, self-contained village; River Street Inn, Ketchum B&B	Lodge Dining Room, elegant atmosphere, great service; Trail Creek Cabin, top lunch or dinner sleighride; Pioneer Saloon, bustle and big portions; Barsotti's, Italian with a great mountain view	Après-ski, elegance in the Lodge's Duchin Room, noise at Whiskey Jacques or Slavey's; the best town library in skidom

Resort	Lodging	Dining	Other
Maine Sugarloaf/USA	Sugarloaf Mountain Hotel, spacious modern rooms, walk to lifts; Sugarloafers Ski Dorm, terrific budget dorm; Inn on Winter's Hill (Kingfield), lovely hilltop mansion, now a fine inn	Gepetto's and Gladstone, light lunch to full dinner, easy access; Papillon and One Stanley Avenue (Kingfield), fine French fare	The Bag and Gondola Bar, two good après-ski spots
New Hampshire Ski 93 Bretton Woods	Bretton Arms, small landmark inn, recently restored; Forest Cottages, and Rosebrook, ski-in, ski-out condos	Bretton Arms Dining Room; Fabyan's Station, Italian fare in restored railroad station	Touring Center, exceptional 100-km cross-country trail system
Cannon Mountain	Charlie Lovett's, Franconia Inn, Horse and Hound, Rivagale Inn, and Sugar Hill Inn, a quintet of delightful New England lodges in Franconia	Again, Lovett's, Franconia, Horse and Hound, Rivagale, and Sugar Hill, fine dining in charming settings; Fabyan's Station, Italian fare in converted railroad station	New England Ski Museum, nostalgia at the tram base
Loon Mountain	Mountain Club on Loon, hotel at ski area base; Indian Head Resort, lots of activities; Alpine Village (North Woodstock), attractive townhouses; Charpentier's (Lincoln), B&B	Rachel's, good hotel restaurant; Common Man (Lincoln), American country fare; Clement Room and Woodstock Station, Woodstock Inn (North Woodstock), two dining options; Tavern at the Mill, modern menu in old mill setting	North Conway outlet shopping, a half-hour drive via the Kancamagus Highway; Mountain Club Fitness Center
Waterville Valley	Snowy Owl Inn, suites in the new wing are great; Black Bear, new condo-hotel; Campton Inn, New England classic lodge	O'Keefe's, good seafood and other favorites; Valley Inn and Tavern, elegant dining; Carnevale's (Campton), northern Italian; Mad River Tavern, American cuisine	Excellent ski-touring facilities; with 100 km of trails
New Mexico Taos Ski Valley	Edelweiss, St. Bernard, Hondo, and Thunderbird, traditional lodges at the base; Taos Inn, charm and history in town; Quail Ridge Inn, top condos between town and mountain	St. Bernard, tops for French fare and friendly service; Casa Cordova, fine Italian cuisine in old hacienda; Apple Tree, international menu, in town; Comidas del Mantes, lucullian portions of home-cooked Mexican	Day or evening in Taos, to dine well, shop, gallery hop; Millicent Rogers Museum, Indian and Spanish colonial art; Taos Pueblo; Kit Carson Home

Resort	Lodging	Dining	Other
Utah Little Cottonwood	Alta Lodge, one of skidom's best, most congenial inns; Rustler Lodge (Alta), larger, more opulently appointed Alta classic; Cliff Lodge (Snowbird), high-rise with spacious, modern rooms and full hotel services	Shallow Shaft (Alta), seafood, steak, and mining memorabilia; Cliff Dining Room (Snowbird), elegant atmosphere; Aerie, retro-Deco look and great views; Mexican Keyhole, spicy bargains	Cliff spa, two-story fitness and beauty center, the best in the West; Wasatch Powderbird Guides, day trips to the Wasatch and Uintas
Park City and Deer Valley	Imperial Hotel, Snowed Inn, and Washington School Inn (Park City), antique-filled charmers; Resort Center and Shadow Ridge, best located condos, walk to Park City lifts; Stein Eriksen Lodge and Stag Lodge (Deer Valley), new luxury lodges	In Park City, Adolph's, luxury continental; Claimjumper and Grub Stake, beef and other hearties; Utah Coal & Lumber, casual Tex-Mex tradition At Deer Valley, Phillippe's and Cafe Mariposa, elegance and exemplary cuisine	Resort Center rink, outdoor skating; lunch at Deer Valley; Utah Interconnect, guided excursion to five ski areas in three valleys; locally brewed Wasatch beer
Vermont Killington	Mountain Inn and Cortina Inn, contemporary luxury; Chalet Killington, well-appointed B&B; Killington Village, condos close to skiing; Red Clover Inn, country style; Mountaintop Inn (Chittendon), services, views, and own touring center	Annabelle's (Stockbridge), casual elegance; Bentley's (Woodstock), gourmet Victorian; Casey's Caboose, steaks and seafood stop on access road; Charity's, pub food; Grist Mill, New England farmhouse atmosphere and American fare	Red Rob, Pickel Barrel, and Wobbly Barn, top after-ski spots; one half-hour drive to Woodstock, shopping and dining
Stowe	Topnotch, luxury and service; Inn at the Mountain, modern, convenient; Edson Hill Manor, Fiddler's Green Inn, and Ten Acres Lodge, charming old inns; Trapp Family Lodge, *Sound of Music* ambiance	Charda, Hungarian specials; Swisspot, Alpine specials and casual fare; The Shed, huge eclectic menu; Ten Acres, creativity from the kitchen	Winter Carnival, one of the best; cross-country at four fine centers; custom order a wool ski hat from Moriarty's
Wyoming Jackson Hole	Alpenhof, Inn at Jackson Hole, and Sojourner Inn, tops at Teton Village; Wort Hotel, restored downtown Jackson; Jackson Hole Racquet Club and Spring Creek Ranch, luxury condos away from town and mountain; Silver King, large resort hotel with own ski hill	Stiegler's, Austro-elegance; The Granary at Spring Creek, fine food and finer views; La Chispa, casual Mexican; Cadillac Grille, retro look and trendy fare	Snowmobile to Old Faithful; sleighride to the National Elk Refuge; party at the Million Dollar Cowboy Bar or Silver Dollar Bar at the Wort

Black-and-White Photo Credits

Early years: p. 15 Lewis Collection/Ketchum Community Library; p. 17 Sun Valley Photo; p. 18 Cross Collection/Ketchum Community Library.
Aspen p. 21 Snowmass Lodging Co.; p. 22 Snowmass Resort Assn. Photo.
Jackson Hole: pp. 29, 30 Jerry LeBlond.
Killington: p. 35 Jerry LeBlond.
Lake Tahoe: pp. 43, 45 Chaco Mohler/Mountain Stock; p. 46 Alpine Meadows Photo.
Park City Areas: p. 54 Scott Nelson/Deer Valley Photo; p. 55 Deer Valley Photo.
Ski 93: p. 62 Bob Grant/Loon Mountain Photo; p. 64 Joan Eaton/Waterville Valley Photo.
Ski the Summit: p. 68 Jeff Andrew/Keystone Photo.
Snowbird/Alta: p. 78 Brian Robb; p. 79 Brian Robb/Snowbird Photo; p. 99 Chaco Mohler/Mountain Stock.
Steamboat: pp. 103, 104, 105 Steamboat Ski Corp.

Stowe: p. 110 (l) Stowe Ski Area Photo; (r) Jerry LeBlond.
Sugarloaf: p. 119 Sugarloaf Photo.
Sun Valley: pp. 125, 126 David Stoecklein; p. 127 UP Collection/Ketchum Community Library.
Taos: pp. 134, 139 David Stoecklein.
Telluride: pp. 142, 143 Chaco Mohler/Mountain Stock.
Vail: pp. 149, 151 David Lokey/Vail Photos; p. 152 Vail Photo
Winter Park: p. 160 Bruce Barthel/Winter Park Photo; p. 177 Chaco Mohler/Mountain Stock.
Best of the Rest/East: p. 184 Jerry LeBlond; p. 187 Snowshoe Mountain Resort Photo.
Best of the Rest/West: p. 193 Mammoth Ski Resort Photo.
Heli/Skiing: pp. 197, 200 Peter Wingle/CMH Heli-skiing Photos.
Lake Louise: p. 204 CP Hotels Photo.
Whistler/Blackcomb: p. 212 Chaco Mohler/Mountain Stock.

Color Photo Credits

Aspen: p. 81 Brian Robb; p. 82 (top) Brian Robb; (bottom) Snowmass Photo.
Jackson Hole: All photos by Jerry LeBlond.
Killington: All photos by Jerry LeBlond.
Lake Tahoe: p. 85 (l) Vance Fox/Mountain Stock; (r, top) Lori Adamski-Peek/Alpine Meadows Photo; (r, center & bottom) Chaco Mohler/Mountain Stock.
Park City areas: p. 86 DeerValley Photo; p. 87 All photos by Chaco Mohler/Mountain Stock.
Ski 93: p. 88 (l, top) Bob Grant/Loon Mountain Photo; (r, top) Jerry LeBlond; (bottom), Joan Eaton/Waterville Valley Photo.
Ski the Summit: p. 89 (top) Jeff Andrew/Copper Mountain Photo; (l, bottom), Breckenridge Photo; (r, bottom), Keystone Photo.
Snowbird/Alta: p. 90 Ed Blankman/Snowbird Photo; p. 91 (l) David Stoecklein; (r) Snowbird Photo.
Steamboat: All photos Steamboat Ski Corp.
Stowe: p. 94 (l) Mount Mansfield at Stowe Photo; (r, top) Stowe Ski Area Photo; (r, bottom) Jerry LeBlond.
Sugarloaf: p. 95 (top) Chip Carey/Sugarloaf Photo; other photos by David Brownell/Sugarloaf Photos.
Sun Valley: p. 161 David Stoecklein; p. 162 Jack Williams/Sun Valley Photo; p. 163 (top) Jack Williams/Sun Valley Photo; (bottom) David Stoecklein.

Taos: All photos by David Stoecklein.
Telluride: p. 165 (l) Chaco Mohler/Mountain Stock; (r, top) Linda Waidhoffer/Telluride Photo; (r, bottom) Robert Hagan/Telluride Photo.
Vail/Beaver Creek: p. 166 Rod Walker/Mountain Stock; p. 167 (l, top) David Lokey/Beaver Creek Photo; (l, bottom) Brian Robb; (r, top) Brian Robb; (r, bottom) Chaco Mohler/Mountain Stock.
Winter Park: p. 168 Winter Park Photo; p. 169 (l) John Kennedy/Winter Park; (r) Chaco Mohler/Mountain Stock.
Best of the Rest/East: p. 170 (top) Jerry LeBlond; (bottom) Mont Sainte Anne Photo.
Best of the Rest/West: p. 171 (l, top) Crested Butte Mountain Resort Photo; (r, top) Brian Robb; (l, bottom) Grand Targhee Photo; (r, bottom) Big Sky Photo.
Heli/Skiing: p. 172 Peter Wingle/CMH Heli-skiing; p. 173 (top) Gary Brettnacher/CMH Heli-skiing; (bottom), Guy Clarkson/CMH Heli-skiing.
Lake Louise: p. 174 CP Hotels Photos; p. 175 Chaco Mohler/Mountain Stock.
Whistler/Blackcomb: All photos by Chaco Mohler/Mountain Stock.